The Vilcek Foundation honors immigrants' extraordinary contributions to America. We, the Foundation's President and Culinary Projects Director, spent the past two years getting to know the country's leading foreign-born chefs and in early 2018 put out a national call for applications for our second cycle of culinary prizes. To help choose the winners, we met with some of the country's leading restaurant critics, food writers, and top chefs to identify the enormously talented immigrants who are transforming American culinary culture from coast to coast.

In 2019, we presented $250,000 in prizes to four immigrants in the culinary arts, but we decided to honor many more. What you hold in your hands is the result: a celebration of forty of the leading foreign-born chefs in the United States, including three of our winners, many other lauded leaders, and dozens of rising stars who are changing American food—for the better.

—Rick Kinsel & Gabrielle Langholtz

EDITED BY
RICK KINSEL &
GABRIELLE LANGHOLTZ

A PLACE AT THE TABLE

NEW AMERICAN RECIPES FROM THE NATION'S TOP FOREIGN-BORN CHEFS

VILCEK FOUNDATION

PRESTEL
MUNICH
LONDON
NEW YORK

Contents

04 Foreword by José Andrés

06 Introduction by Padma Lakshmi

09 Fariyal Abdullahi

15 Tatsu Aikawa

21 Emma Bengtsson

29 Erik Bruner-Yang

35 Maneet Chauhan

43 Dominique Crenn

49 Thai Dang

55 Carlos Delgado

61 Hugue Dufour

67 Diego Galicia

73 Cesar Gutierrez

79 Jae-Eun Jung

87 Ann Kim

91 Carlo Lamagna

97 Corey Lee

103 Edward Lee

107 Johnny Lee

113 Binhong Lu

117 Daniela Moreira

123 Vansana Nolintha

129 Charles Olalia

135 Pichet Ong

141 Hugo Ortega

147 Laura and Sayat Ozyilmaz

153 Norberto Piattoni

159 Marcus Samuelsson

167 Peter Serpico

173 Alon Shaya

177 Michael Solomonov

183 Mutsuko Soma

189 Daniela Soto-Innes

195 Joseph Sukhendra

201 Kate Telfeyan

207 Simone Tong

213 Miroslav Uskokovic

221 Harold Villarosa

227 Fabián von Hauske Valtierra

235 Shuai Wang

241 Tunde Wey

245 Nite Yun

250 Index

255 Acknowledgments & Credits

Foreword

José Andrés

Founder,
World Central Kitchen

Winner,
2010 Vilcek Prize
in Culinary Arts

I am an immigrant and I am an American. I was born and raised in Spain and, after living in the United States for more than twenty years, was granted American citizenship alongside my wife. Many, many of us come from other places, and for those of us who were born here, our parents or grandparents or great-grandparents came from somewhere else (except, of course, those who have always been on this land). This is one of the most beautiful things about America—we are a nation of people from around the globe who bring our own stories, our own culture, and our own histories to this country. Immigrants make America—we are woven into the history of the country from before its founding. We are deep in its DNA.

I am also a cook. I see the world from behind a stove. Many of us immigrants have found our way into kitchens and restaurants—the restaurant industry is a welcoming place for us to land. Kitchens are a sort of United Nations in miniature: everyone may speak a different language and has grown up with different spices, but we all have the same goals, the same dreams, the same desire to nourish everyone that comes in for a meal. Each of the chefs profiled in this cookbook has seen what I see: a vibrant, multicultural community that comes together every night to make and serve the best food they possibly can, from the dishwashers to the line cooks to the bartenders to the head chef. It is deeply inspiring, and deeply humbling, to be a part of this community.

And what are we cooking in our kitchens? The food we make in America today is a reflection of ourselves, of the complexities of building a new home far from where we were born. We will often adapt our recipes to the ingredients that we can find locally, and maybe adjust our dishes to be more suitable for local palates. We create new flavor combinations to make food that has our own accents, representing our hyphenated natures. In the end, it can all be considered *American food*—it is the creation of generations of immigrants representing waves of migration from all around the world. Today, sushi, kebabs, and tacos are just as important for American cuisine as burgers, pizza, and meatloaf.

There are forces in our country that view immigrants as a danger and immigration as a problem—forces of exclusion hoping to drive the nation apart. To me, immigration is not a problem to solve but an opportunity to seize, and each and every one of us can benefit. My restaurants never have enough people—we are always having trouble hiring—and I know this issue is shared by many of my peers in the industry, as well as in agriculture, hospitality, and other industries that employ immigrants. So instead of turning people away at the borders, or keeping undocumented immigrants in the shadows, why don't we welcome them into our workforce? This sort of thinking not only helps our restaurants, our farms, and our hotels, but also adds to the rich tapestry of our nation.

I am proud to be an immigrant, and I am proud to be an American. And I am proud to have been honored with the inaugural Vilcek Prize in Culinary Arts—and to have used the prize money to help found World Central Kitchen, which uses food as an agent of change. I believe that all the diversity, all the voices, and all the stories from around the world make America better—we are the greatest nation on earth, stronger and more creative, braver and less fearful because of who we are. The forty immigrant chefs profiled in this cookbook and the hundreds of thousands of immigrants who work in the restaurant industry around the country are key to making America—and American food—great. Explore this book and the amazing recipes collected here and you will quickly see: we all have a place at the table.

Introduction
Immigration Is Delicious

Padma Lakshmi

Host & Executive Producer,
Top Chef

I am an immigrant.

I came here when I was four to join my mother, a nurse who had emigrated from India two years earlier. She'd had exactly $100 in her pocket when she left a turbulent marriage for the United States and willed a new life for us into existence. I love this country for allowing that to be possible for her and for me—along with so many others. America has shaped my family's dreams and values.

I was lucky to grow up in New York, a city of immigrants. For many, it's a microcosm of the most idealized version of this country. My neighbors were Peruvian and Filipino, doctors, nurses, line cooks, and cab drivers. These people were the heartbeat of my beloved city. As a kid I used to roller skate all over the streets of New York, and seeing all these faces from around the world showed me that I belonged here, too. In those days in the '70s, most of the Indian markets were in the borough of Queens. We lived in Manhattan. My mother and I would travel uptown to Spanish Harlem for things like tamarind and sugar cane and all the way downtown to Chinatown for vegetables like bitter gourd and lotus stem and for spices like star anise and black cardamom.

In our quest for our own ingredients, we would bump up against other immigrant communities. These folks had much to tell us, not only about how they eat but also about how they live and what they value. The city became my first culinary playground. It set the stage for a lifelong passion to connect with communities by sharing their foods with them. The city lit my young palate on fire and I have been tasting the world ever since through my fork.

My mother and I had little extra money for fine dining in those days. We were mostly going to pupusa stands and falafel joints, delicious but not exactly white-tablecloth establishments. Today, there is a whole cornucopia of foods brought here from all over the world, at every level of dining. These days, you don't have to turn to food trucks to encounter diversity of cuisines (though those are some of *my* favorite places to discover new treats). You can enjoy the highest levels of Mexican gastronomy from people like Daniela Soto-Innes at Cosme and Atla, a place I love for neighborhood brunch. You can savor the delicious results that come from a comingling of Ethiopian and Swedish food through the genius of chefs like my friend Marcus Samuelsson, who does high and humble cuisine with equal ease. You can amaze your sweet tooth with the innovative desserts of Serbian pastry chef Miro Uskokovic at Gramercy Tavern, who shows us that not all sugar is created equal by using ingredients like Bangladeshi date jaggery. His is a custard I can get behind!

Through my work on *Top Chef*, I've had the chance to meet people all over America. I've lived on both coasts and have also spent lots of time in cities like Charleston, Louisville, Seattle, Chicago, New Orleans, and Miami. What makes all of these places great is the diversity of the people who call them home. This diversity makes our history richer, our art more vibrant, and our food so much more interesting and delicious. I've had the best *banh mi*, or Vietnamese po boy, at the family-owned Pho Tau Bay in New Orleans, lip smacking *chaat* to rival street stalls in New Delhi by Maneet Chauhan in both Chicago and Nashville, the seamless fusion (yes, *fusion*! It's not a dirty word, but a delicious one!) of authentic Southern food with true Korean flavors from Ed Lee in Kentucky. These craveable things are all possible because this is who we are as Americans. Immigrants have not only built a national culinary palate, we've built this very nation. Every one of us, all of us, over many generations, since the first wave came to Plymouth Rock.

At its best, our country has been admired as a beacon of hope because of our tradition of welcoming people from all around the world and from all walks of life. Whether they're white or brown, gay or straight, male or female, a person can come here and create a new life and new art forms. That's the American dream.

I believe what truly makes America great is our culture of inclusion. We are a superpower not because of capitalism or our military. Those things can vastly fluctuate over a nation's history. It's because we've managed to take the best of each immigrant culture over time and create our own uniquely American culture. We've distilled the ethos of a meritocracy based on the value of what each of us brings to the table. And there should be a place at this table for all of us. That's what makes us a vibrant society.

Now I'm a mother myself. I want my daughter to live in a country whose foods are delicious and diverse (even more so than when I grew up) and whose policies aren't governed by fear, but by compassion. A country that teaches all our children the very American principles of empathy, inclusion, and opportunity.

We are the United States of America. Let's remember who we are, which is spelled out in the first word of our country's name: United.

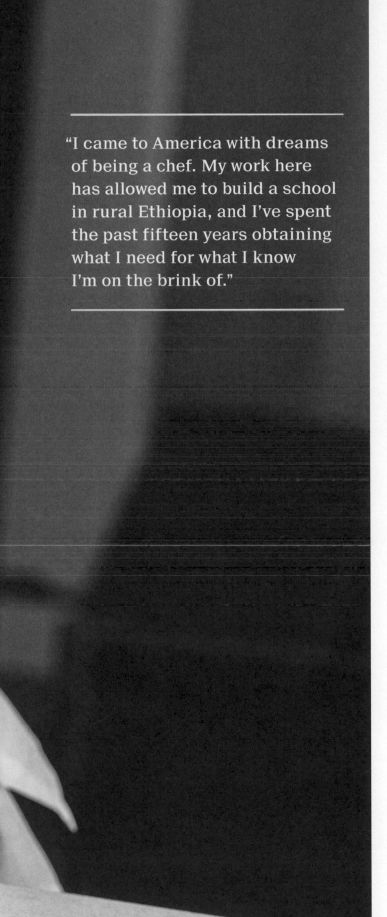

Ethiopia ⟶ Dallas, Texas

Fariyal Abdullahi

"I came to America with dreams of being a chef. My work here has allowed me to build a school in rural Ethiopia, and I've spent the past fifteen years obtaining what I need for what I know I'm on the brink of."

Growing up in Ethiopia, Fariyal Abdullahi developed a passion for cooking while helping her mother cook food for eight people daily. But to make her mother proud, she followed her sisters' footsteps into medicine and, at age seventeen, moved to the United States to study clinical psychology.

After obtaining her bachelor's, Abdullahi secretly applied not to grad school, but to the Culinary Institute of America. While waiting to hear back, she ate her way around the world. In three months, she covered eighteen countries, and formed an unshakable commitment to pursuing her dream career as a chef. Back in the US, she learned that she had been accepted to culinary school. With her mother's blessing, she moved to Napa Valley to attend the CIA, where she received three scholarships. From there she applied to Noma in Copenhagen, widely regarded as the best restaurant in the world, and was accepted.

Abdullahi moved to Copenhagen for her internship at Noma, where she cooked for legendary chefs from around the world at Noma's Mad Symposium. Upon returning to the US, she joined Hillstone Restaurant Group and, after a year with the company, was made head of her own kitchen as Culinary Manager.

She says cooking can help people and the planet, which is the legacy she'd like to leave.

Fariyal Abdullahi

Teff Pancakes

Serves 4

Teff is an ancient grain that is native to Ethiopia. Central to the country's cuisine, it is cooked into the giant, thin pancakes known as injera on which most Ethiopian meals are served. In this riff, teff flour—the milled form of the grain—is cooked into sweet pancakes to serve at breakfast. Teff is nutritious, delicious, and naturally gluten-free.

2 cups (320 g) teff flour
1 tablespoon ground cardamom
1 tablespoon baking powder
1 tablespoon granulated sugar
½ teaspoon salt
1 overripe banana
1½ cups (360 ml) almond milk
½ tablespoon vanilla extract
Butter or oil, for oooking the pancakes
Seasonal fruit and maple syrup, for serving

In a large bowl, whisk together the teff flour, cardamom, baking powder, sugar, and salt. In a small bowl, mash the banana. Add the almond milk and vanilla and stir until combined then add to the teff flour mixture and stir until combined.

Heat a skillet or griddle over medium-high heat and lightly coat with butter or oil. Working in batches, add about ¼ cup (60 ml) of batter per pancake and cook for about 2½ minutes or until the edges turn a darker brown and the batter stops bubbling. Flip the pancakes and cook for about 2½ minutes longer or until they bounce back when pressed with a spatula. Repeat with the remaining batter to make more pancakes, adding more butter or oil as needed. Serve with fruit and maple syrup.

Fariyal Abdullahi

Coffee-Braised Short Ribs

Serves 4

The coffee plant originated in Ethiopia, which remains Africa's top coffee producer. This recipe uses cold brew coffee as a flavorful braising liquid. The ribs can be made up to three days ahead and reheated gently at serving time.

4 boneless or bone-in short ribs,
    6 ounces to ½ pound
    (170 to 225 g) each
Salt and freshly ground pepper
2 tablespoons olive oil
4 celery stalks, cut into large dice
2 carrots, cut into large dice
1 medium yellow onion,
    cut into large dice
2 tablespoons tomato paste
1 cup (240 ml) pomegranate juice
2 cups (480 ml) beef stock
1 cup (240 ml) cold brew coffee
1 whole head garlic,
    halved crosswise
5 sprigs fresh thyme
3 bay leaves
Polenta or whipped potatoes,
    for serving

Generously season the ribs with salt and pepper. In a large braising pot or Dutch oven, heat the olive oil over medium-high heat. Add the ribs and cook, turning frequently, until golden brown all over. Transfer the ribs to a plate, but leave the pot on the heat. Add the celery, carrots, and onion and cook, stirring, for 5 to 7 minutes or until golden.

Add the tomato paste and cook for about 2 minutes or until it darkens and starts to smell sweet. Add the pomegranate juice and bring to a boil, scraping up any browned bits from the bottom of the pot. Return the ribs to the pot then add the beef stock, cold brew coffee, garlic, thyme, and bay leaves. Bring to a boil over high heat, then reduce the heat to medium low, cover, and cook for about 1½ hours or until the ribs are tender. Serve hot with polenta or whipped potatoes.

Japan ⟶ Austin, Texas

Tatsu
Aikawa

Tatsu Aikawa brought ramen culture and izakaya-style dining to Austin. He's Tokyo-born and Texas-bred, and his food is rooted in Japanese traditions while evoking the spirit and smoke of his adopted state.

Aikawa's father ran a restaurant in Tokyo but his parents divorced and when he was ten, his mother moved them to the United States through a cultural exchange program. Later on, to help her pay the bills, he found work as a dishwasher and eventually worked his way up to executive chef. An apprenticeship with Michelin-starred sushi chef Hiroyuki Urasawa took him to Los Angeles, and it was during this time that Aikawa was inspired to perfect recipes for his own ramen-ya. He moved back to Austin in 2012, intent on educating Texans that there's more to Japanese cuisine than sushi, and opened Ramen Tatsu-ya, the city's first brick-and-mortar ramen noodle restaurant. Aikawa's second venture was an izakaya, with a smoker out front producing brisket and ribs as well as smoked fish. Opened in 2017, Kemuri Tatsu-ya earned instant acclaim, including a spot on *Bon Appétit*'s Hot Ten list of Best New Restaurants 2017 and as a James Beard Foundation Semi-Finalist for Best New Restaurant 2018. Aikawa has aspirations for more ramen shops, as well as an intimate omakase counter, where he will continue to combine Tokyo soul with Texas heart.

"I wanted to do something I love for a living, I felt that was my ultimate freedom. I smoke fish, but I also make brisket. Essentially my food is a story of me, a Japanese kid who grew up in Texas."

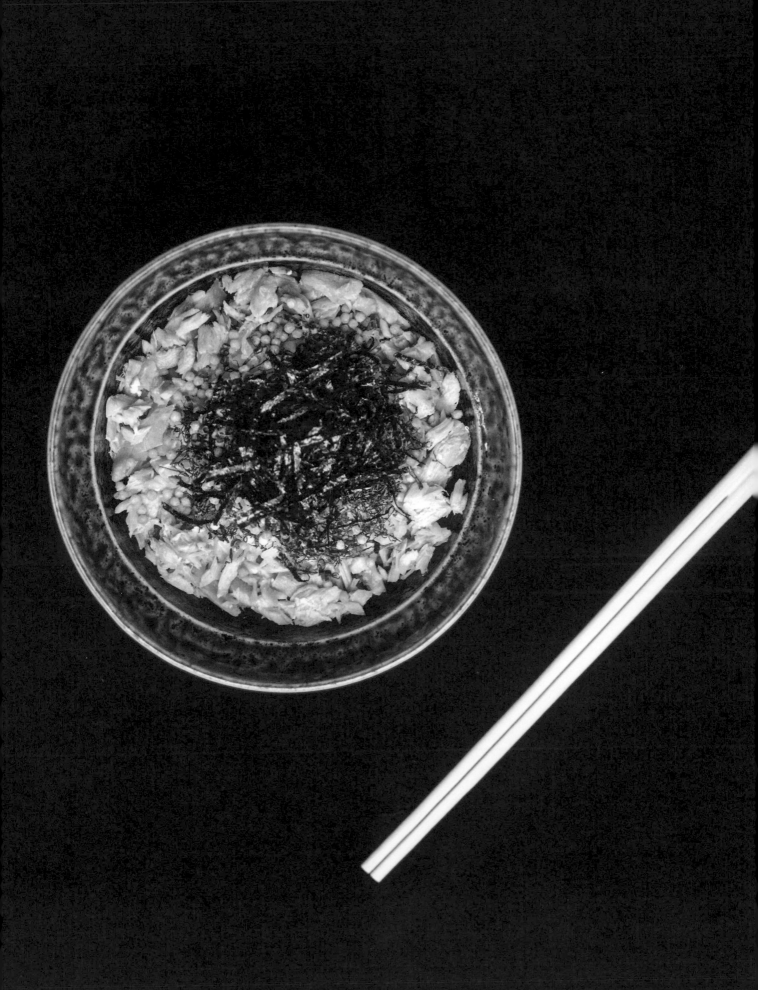

Tatsu Aikawa

Ochazuke

Ochazuke Is a simple dish of green tea poured over rice— *ocha* means "tea" and *zuke* means "to submerge"—but if you have a piece of salted fish and a pickle, you can make yourself a quick meal. I have many memories of eating ochazuke growing up. My mom was a single, working parent, and this was an easy recipe that I could make myself at home. It also reminds me of my grandma, who drank a lot of green tea. When I make this, I see her face.

There are many variations of ochazuke, but this is a dashi version, which you usually find at *kappo-* or *kaiseki*-style restaurants. The salmon is meant to be slightly oversalted, as the broth is underseasoned—make sure you season the dashi just lightly with soy sauce. Also, washing the rice after it's cooked is crucial for the texture of the dish. It removes extra starch, giving the rice a more al dente mouthfeel.

For the salmon
1 (2-ounce / 60-g) piece skinless
    salmon
¼ cup (60 ml) sake
½ teaspoon salt
Canola oil

For the dashi
1 (3-inch / 7.5-cm) piece kombu
    (preferably Ma-Konbu, Rishiri,
    or Rausu)
2 cups plus 1 tablespoon (495 ml)
    water
¾ ounce (20 g) katsuobushi
    (bonito flakes)
¼ teaspoon salt
Soy sauce, preferably white shoyu,
    to taste

For serving
½ cup (100 g) Japanese rice, cooked
Nori strips, crumbled rice
    crackers, grated wasabi, shiso
    leaf ribbons, thin fresh yuzu or
    lemon rind strips, and minced
    chives, for garnish
Asazuke Pickles (recipe p. 19),
    for serving

For the salmon
Massage the fish all over with the sake and salt. Wrap it in plastic wrap and refrigerate overnight.

Light a grill or preheat a small cast-iron pan over medium-high heat. Very lightly oil the grill grates or cast-iron pan with canola oil if needed to prevent sticking. Add the salmon and grill or cook, turning once, for about 4 minutes or until cooked through. Transfer to a plate and let cool.

For the dashi
Clean the kombu with a damp towel, leaving as much of the white powder as possible. In a medium pot, cover the kombu with 2 cups (480 ml) of the water and let stand for 30 minutes. Set the pot over medium-high heat and cook until the kombu floats to the top then remove the kombu and bring the liquid to a rolling boil. Add the remaining 1 tablespoon of water to calm the boil then add the katsuobushi. Return to a boil then lower the heat and simmer for 2 minutes. Remove from the heat, skim any foam from the dashi, and let stand until the katsuobushi falls to the bottom. Line a strainer with a paper towel and set over a clean saucepan.

Strain the dashi through the paper towel. Add the salt and season lightly with soy sauce.

For serving
Rinse the cooked rice in cold water for 10 to 20 seconds to remove excess starch then drain and arrange in 2 bowls. Tear the cooled salmon into pieces and arrange on top of the rice. Garnish with nori strips, rice crackers, wasabi, shiso, yuzu or lemon rind, and chives. To finish, gently warm the dashi if needed and pour it into the bowls until it covers all of the rice. Serve with Asazuke Pickles.

Tatsu Aikawa

Asazuke Pickles

Serves 2

In Japanese cooking, we love pickled vegetables and put them in everything. This simple cabbage-based pickle is a perfect side for rice.

¼ pound (110 g) green cabbage
¼ teaspoon salt
½ Japanese cucumber (or 1 whole Persian cucumber), sliced
¼ carrot, sliced
1 teaspoon julienned fresh ginger plus grated fresh ginger for garnish
2 teaspoons rice vinegar
1½ teaspoons dried kombu tea (not brewed)
¾ teaspoon soy sauce
White sesame seeds and Katsuobushi (bonito flakes), for garnish

Rinse the cabbage then cut it into bite-size pieces and place in a large bowl. Add the salt and massage it into the cabbage. Add the cucumber, carrot, and julienned ginger and mix well.

Transfer the vegetables to a resealable plastic bag, add the rice vinegar, kombu tea, and soy sauce then seal the bag, squeezing out any excess air. Massage the bag for 2 to 3 minutes or until the vegetables are slightly soft. Refrigerate for 30 to 45 minutes to fully marinate the vegetables.

Transfer the vegetables to a serving bowl then garnish with the sesame seeds, katsuobushi, and grated ginger and serve. The pickles can be refrigerated for up to 1 week.

Sweden ⟶ New York, New York

Emma Bengtsson

Emma Bengtsson first learned to cook from her grandmother in western Sweden, and went on to become the second woman in the US to run a two-Michelin-starred kitchen. She graduated from culinary school first in her class of 650 students, then worked in the kitchens of some of Stockholm's most lauded restaurants, including Restaurant Prinsen, Operakällaren, and Edsbacka Krog, the only restaurant in Sweden with two Michelin stars at the time.

Arriving in New York City with a one-year work visa and a dream to share modern Scandinavian cuisine with a new world, Bengtsson became the executive pastry chef at Aquavit in 2010. There she established a new bread program and gained acclaim for her beautifully rendered desserts, including the Arctic Bird's Nest, a goat cheese parfait "egg" with white chocolate shell and sea buckthorn curd "yolk," nestled in a crisp pastry and surrounded by a wilderness-inspired tangle of berries, blossoms, and tender shoots with a dusting of frozen yogurt "snow." Her work as ambassador of high-end Swedish cuisine has garnered a three-star review in the *New York Times*, helped land Aquavit its second Michelin star, and made her a semifinalist for the James Beard Award for Best Chef: New York City.

Now the executive chef at Aquavit, Bengtsson uses her role to advocate for women in the culinary field and to address childhood hunger through City Harvest and No Kid Hungry.

"America has always been the land of opportunity for Swedish people, who first came here generations ago as refugees from pain and misery back home. The US is a country where we can become better, and have a better quality of life. So living and working here was always a dream to me.

The diversity of foods from around the world is quite fantastic and amazing. Culinarily, America is a no-rule land, where you can take your cuisine and mix it with everything else, influenced by so many different cuisines. When you start creating, everything you see around you is in your heart and mind, and all the ingredients from across the states. It's incredible."

Emma Bengtsson

Gravlax with Watermelon, Cucumber, Peas, and Lovage

Gravlax is very close to my heart, one of my favorite things to eat, and always on the menu. I like to recreate it in different ways as the seasons change. It's very important to me. This version is a very fresh summer dish that might look hard to recreate, but if you have a little time, you can make it at home and impress your guests.

Use any leftover frozen-melon vinaigrette as a refreshing addition to salads or alongside sliced melon.

For the gravlax
2 cups (400 g) granulated sugar
2 cups (400 g) kosher salt
1 bunch fresh dill, finely chopped
¼ cup (40 g) white peppercorns
½ side of salmon, about 1 pound
    (450 g) total, skinned

For the frozen melon vinaigrette
¼ watermelon, about 1¼ pounds
    (560 g) total, rind removed and
    cut into small pieces
3 celery stalks, roughly chopped
3 green apples, peeled
    and roughly chopped
1 bunch fresh lovage
2 tablespoons maple syrup
Juice of 2 lemons
2 teaspoons distilled white vinegar
Kosher salt

For the cucumber cubes
¼ cup (60 ml) distilled white vinegar
¼ cup (60 ml) water
¼ cup (50 g) granulated sugar
½ carrot
½ onion
½ parsnip
1 (1-ounce / 28-g) piece
    fresh horseradish
2 tablespoons black peppercorns
1 bay leaf
1 English cucumber,
    cut into small dice

For the watermelon cubes
¼ watermelon, about 1¼ pounds
    (560 g) total, rind removed and
    cut into small dice
½ cup (120 ml) elderflower syrup
Juice of 1 lemon
Kosher salt

For the English peas
6 ounces (170 g) English peas in the
    pod, shelled (½ cup shelled)
Juice of 1 lemon
Kosher salt

For serving
4 small radishes, thinly sliced
Salmon roe (optional)
20 fresh chive or dill blossoms
20 fresh sorrel leaves

For the gravlax
In a large bowl, combine the sugar, kosher salt, dill, and white peppercorns. Spread ½ of the cure mixture on the bottom of a baking dish that's 4 inches deep (10 cm) and large enough to fit the salmon. Place the salmon on top and cover with the rest of the cure mixture. Cover and refrigerate for forty eight hours, flipping the salmon every 12 hours or so and making sure it stays fully covered in the cure mixture. Discard the curing mixture and rinse the salmon under cold water.

For the frozen melon vinaigrette
In a food processor or blender, purée the watermelon, celery, apples, lovage, and maple syrup until smooth. Add the lemon juice, distilled white vinegar, and a scant teaspoon of kosher salt and pulse to incorporate. Let stand at room temperature for 10 to 20 minutes then strain through a coffee filter or paper towel into a shallow, freezer-safe baking dish. Freeze for 30 to 60 minutes or until ice crystals form around the edges. With a fork, scrape the crystals to the center of the baking dish then return to the freezer and repeat every 30 minutes for 2 to 3 hours or until all of the liquid is crystalized but not frozen solid.

Continued ⟶

Emma Bengtsson

For the cucumber cubes

In a medium saucepan, bring the distilled white vinegar, water, and sugar to a boil, stirring until the sugar is dissolved. Remove from the heat and add the carrot, onion, parsnip, horseradish, black peppercorns, and bay leaf and let stand for 30 minutes. Strain liquid.

Place the cucumber in a medium bowl or a large glass jar, add the pickling liquid, cover, and refrigerate for about 2 hours.

For the watermelon cubes

In a medium bowl, toss the watermelon with the elderflower syrup, lemon juice, and a pinch of salt then cover and refrigerate for about 2 hours.

For the English peas

Fill a large bowl with ice water and bring a medium saucepan of salted water to a boil. Blanch the peas for 30 seconds or until al dente. Transfer the peas to the ice water, then remove and discard their skins and place the peas in small a bowl. Dress the peas lightly with lemon juice and salt.

For serving

Cut the gravlax into small dice and divide among 4 bowls. Arrange the watermelon and cucumber cubes around the gravlax. Fill in the spaces with the peas, radishes, and salmon roe, if using. Garnish with chive or dill blossoms and sorrel leaves. Finish each bowl with 2 spoonfuls of the frozen melon vinaigrette and serve immediately.

Emma Bengtsson

Spring Barley and Vegetables

The most beautiful season in New York is early summer, when there are so many wonderful vegetables at the farmers market. Swedish cuisine uses a lot of seafood and wild game, so it's rare to find vegetarian cuisine there, but you don't need animal protein at every meal. This is a bright dish that you can make at home using lots of peas, asparagus, the wild leeks known as ramps, and the first cherry tomatoes of the year.

For the ramp oil
4 cups (70 g) ramp leaves
2 cups (480 ml) canola oil

For the pickled tomatoes
½ cup (120 ml) white distilled vinegar
½ cup (120 ml) water
½ cup (100 g) granulated sugar
1 cup (125 g) cherry tomatoes

For the puffed amaranth
4 cups (960 ml) canola oil
½ cup (105 g) amaranth
Salt

For the barley and spinach purée
2 cups (400 g) pearl barley
6 cups (1.4 l) water
1 bunch thyme
4 garlic cloves, crushed
2 Spanish onions,
    quartered and peeled
8 cups (6 ounces or 150g) spinach
Salt
¼ cup (25 g) grated parmesan
1 tablespoon unsalted butter

For the spring vegetables and spinach purée
¼ pound (100 g) green asparagus,
    peeled and cut into 2-inch (5 cm)
    pieces
¼ pound (100 g) sugar snap peas,
    trimmed and halved on
    the diagonal
¼ pound (100 g) snow peas,
    trimmed and thinly sliced
    crosswise
1 tablespoon unsalted butter
Salt

For serving
Juice of 2 lemons
8 green asparagus stalks,
    shaved lengthwise into ribbons
4 young carrots, shaved lengthwise
    into ribbons
4 radishes, thinly sliced
1 large handful market greens,
    such as pea shoots, sunflower
    sprouts, or edible flowers

For the ramp oil
Fill a large bowl with ice water and bring a medium saucepan of salted water to a boil. Blanch the ramp leaves for 30 seconds or until wilted and bright green. Using tongs, transfer the ramp leaves to the ice water. Once the ramps are cool enough to handle, squeeze them dry.

In a food processor or blender, combine the ramp leaves and canola oil and blend on high speed to get the mixture going, then reduce the speed to medium and blend for 5 minutes or until smooth. Transfer the ramp oil to a resealable container and refrigerate for 24 hours then strain the oil through a coffee filter or paper towel into a jar or bottle and refrigerate until ready to use.

For the pickled tomatoes
Fill a large bowl with ice water and bring a medium saucepan of unsalted water to a boil.

In a small saucepan, bring the white distilled vinegar, water, and sugar to a boil.

Continued ⟶

Emma Bengtsson

Using a paring knife, cut a shallow 'x' at the bottom of each tomato then add the tomatoes to the boiling water and blanch for about 30 seconds or until the skins begin to pull away. Using a slotted ladle or spoon, transfer the tomatoes to the ice water. Once the tomatoes are cool enough to handle, remove and discard their skins and place the tomatoes in a clean 2-cup (480 ml) jar. Pour the pickling liquid over the tomatoes, cover, and refrigerate for about 2 hours.

For the puffed amaranth
In a deep skillet, heat the canola oil until shimmering. Put the amaranth in a fine metal strainer and carefully lower it into the hot oil—the amaranth should puff up almost instantly. Transfer the amaranth to paper towels and season to taste with salt.

For the barley and spinach purée
In a large saucepan, bring the barley and water to a boil. Using kitchen twine, tie the thyme and garlic into a bundle. Add the bundle and the onions to the barley then reduce the heat to medium low, cover, and cook for about 40 minutes or until the barley is soft and the water has been absorbed. Discard the onion, garlic, and thyme.

Meanwhile, fill a large bowl with ice water and bring another large saucepan of salted water to a boil. Add the spinach and blanch for about 10 seconds or until wilted then use tongs to transfer the spinach to the ice water. Once the spinach is cool enough to handle, squeeze it dry and transfer to a food processor or blender. Add ¼ cup (60 ml) of the ice water and a pinch of salt and purée until smooth. Do not let the food processor or blender get too hot or the color of the spinach will turn. Stir the spinach purée into the barley then add the Parmesan and butter, stir, season to taste with salt, and keep warm.

For the spring vegetables
Fill a large bowl with ice water and bring a medium saucepan of salted water to a boil. Add the asparagus and snap peas and blanch for about 1 minute or until crisp-tender. Drain the asparagus and snap peas then transfer to the ice water and drain again. Transfer the asparagus and snap peas to a bowl, add the snow peas, and toss to combine.

In a small skillet, melt the butter over medium heat. Add the asparagus, snap peas, and snow peas and cook until just heated through. Season to taste with salt.

For serving
Season the barley with a little lemon juice and spoon onto 4 plates. Season the spring vegetables with a little lemon juice and spoon on top of the barley. Top each plate with the pickled tomatoes, asparagus and carrot ribbons, and radishes. Sprinkle with the puffed amaranth and drizzle with the ramp oil. Garnish with market greens and serve.

Taiwan ⟶ Washington, DC

Erik Bruner-Yang

"American cuisine is meant to evolve and adapt. I always say I specialize in American cuisine, even though my food represents bold Asian flavors. Asian culture and immigrants have been influential for American pop culture, culinary flavors, and identity since the foundation of the United States."

Born in Taiwan and raised in the United States, Erik Bruner-Yang spent his childhood studying piano and racking up awards at competitions. He was climbing the ranks in the Washington, DC restaurant scene when his grandfather in Taiwan fell ill, and Bruner-Yang began to visit each year, developing a deeper understanding of Taiwanese cuisine. In 2011 he opened Toki Underground, a ramen shop that drew a huge waitlist for its rich broths. Eater DC crowned it Best New Restaurant.

Bruner-Yang has since opened several other DC establishments, including Paper Horse and Maketto. His most recent projects include two venues inside the Line Hotel: Brothers and Sisters, which serves American classics reinterpreted through Taiwanese and Japanese points of view, and Spoken English, modeled after Japanese tachinomiyas or "standing bars" that serve small plates and drinks.

Bruner-Yang was nominated for the James Beard Foundation's Rising Star Chef award in 2015 and was a semifinalist for the Best Chef: Mid-Atlantic award in 2016.

Erik Bruner-Yang

Takoyaki Hush Puppies

Serves 8

My restaurant Brothers and Sisters plays on the idea of an American eatery in a foreign country. Late one night, on a whim, I combined my love of Asian flavors with my even bigger love of American snack food and made these hush puppies inspired by *takoyaki,* a famous Japanese street snack of octopus fried in batter. They're fun to eat, they're fun to say, and it's impossible to have just one. I garnish them with a *tare* sauce, lime mayonnaise, finely diced chives, pickled watermelon radish, and bonito flakes.

1⅓ cups (240 g) semolina flour
1⅓ cups (175 g) all-purpose flour
3 tablespoons garlic powder
3 tablespoons onion powder
1½ teaspoons baking powder
1⅓ teaspoons baking soda
½ teaspoon Korean chili powder
2 cups (480 ml) buttermilk
½ cup (120 ml) sour cream
1 large egg
¼ pound (110 g) chopped cooked octopus
8 scallions, chopped
6 slices bacon, cooked until crispy and chopped
3 tablespoons pickled ginger, finely chopped
Salt and freshly ground pepper
Canola oil

In a large bowl, combine the semolina and all-purpose flours, the garlic powder, onion powder, baking powder, baking soda, and chili powder. Add the buttermilk, sour cream, and egg, followed by the octopus, scallions, bacon, and pickled ginger and stir to combine. Season to taste with salt and pepper. Moisten your hands and form the mixture into roughly 1-inch (2.5 cm) balls.

In a large heavy pot or Dutch oven, bring 3 to 4 inches (7.5 to 10 cm) of canola oil to 350°F (180°C). Set a rack inside a baking sheet and arrange it near the stove. Working in batches of 6, carefully add the balls to the hot oil and fry, turning occasionally, for about 5 minutes or until golden and cooked through. Using a slotted spoon or a strainer with a handle, transfer the hush puppies to the rack to drain and cool slightly. Repeat to fry the remaining hush puppies and serve hot.

Erik Bruner-Yang

Oysters with Uni

Brine on brine. These two ingredients, raw oysters and uni, may seem simple, but when paired together, they pack a fresh ocean punch.

Uni is sea urchin roe and there's nothing like it. You can buy shelled uni, but if it's still in the shell, using kitchen shears, start at the opening and cut until you get halfway down the side, then cut around the perimeter and remove the urchin's lid. These are so easy to prepare and great for either a quiet night at home or as an elegant appetizer that is sure to wow your guests.

6 oysters
6 pieces uni (sea urchin)
Crushed ice, for serving

Shuck the oysters and arrange them on the half shell on a bed of crushed ice. Carefully spoon the uni on top and serve.

India ⟶ Nashville, Tennessee

Maneet Chauhan

Maneet Chauhan grew up in India and graduated from the country's best culinary school at the top of her class. After cooking in some of India's finest kitchens, including the Taj Group, Oberoi Hotels, and Le Meridien, she moved to the US and graduated from the Culinary Institute of America with high honors.

Chauhan beat forty male chefs to become executive chef at the new restaurant Vermilion, overseeing kitchen teams in New York and Chicago. Vermilion was named *Chicago* magazine's Best New Restaurant and *Wine Enthusiast*'s Best New Restaurant in the US, and received rave reviews from *Bon Appétit, USA Today, Time, Esquire, Travel & Leisure, Gourmet, Town & Country, Business Week,* and *O, The Oprah Magazine.*

After eight years leading Vermilion, Chauhan founded Indic Culinaire, a culinary and hospitality company. She was the only Indian female ever to compete on *Iron Chef* and was also a fierce competitor on *The Next Iron Chef*, going on to become a full-time judge on the Food Network show *Chopped*, for which she received a James Beard Award. Chauhan has taught Indian cooking on ABC's *The View* and was chosen to cook at the Indiaspora Inaugural Ball honoring the re-election of President Obama.

Chauhan is the author of a cookbook, *Flavors of My World*. In 2014, she opened Chauhan Ale & Masala House in Nashville.

"American cuisine is the world's largest melting pot because people from all over the world come here, experience new dishes like I did, and combine the fare in entirely new ways. The different cuisines are essentially the fiber of the American tapestry."

Maneet Chauhan

Naanzanella

Naan is a flatbread that's one of the foundations of Indian cuisine. I wanted to pay homage to it by presenting it in a form that's not been seen before. The yogurt dressing is versatile and can be used on other salads and dishes. *Bhel puri* is an Indian snack mix and can be found at Indian markets.

For the mint chutney
2 cups (60 g) fresh cilantro leaves
2 cups (60 g) fresh mint leaves
5 to 6 fresh green chiles, stemmed
1 (½-inch / 1.25-cm) piece fresh
   ginger
1 cup (240 ml) mango pulp
½ cup (120 ml) freshly squeezed
   lime juice
Salt

For the tamarind chutney
¾ cup (180 ml) tamarind water*
¾ cup (50 g) organic dark brown
   sugar (or jaggery, if available)
½ cup (65 g) pitted dates
½ teaspoon cumin seeds, toasted
½ teaspoon fennel seeds
¼ teaspoon chili powder
¼ teaspoon salt

*To make tamarind water, mix 1
tablespoon tamarind
concentrate with ¾ cup (180 ml)
water.

For the naanzanella
Canola oil
4 pieces naan, diced
½ cup (120 ml) plain yogurt
Zest and juice of ½ lemon
Salt
2 cups (330 g) thinly sliced
   strawberries
1 large handful bhel puri
Edible flowers (optional)

For the mint chutney
In a food processor, pulse together the cilantro, mint, green chiles, and ginger until finely chopped. Add the mango pulp and lime juice and purée into a smooth but not homogenous paste. Season to taste with salt. Set aside ¼ cup (60 ml). The leftover chutney can be refrigerated and should be used within 1 or 2 days.

For the tamarind chutney
In a small saucepan, combine the tamarind water, organic dark brown sugar, pitted dates, cumin seeds, fennel seeds, chili powder, and salt and bring to a boil. Lower the heat and simmer, stirring occasionally, for 8 to 10 minutes or until reduced to a thick liquid. Remove from the heat and let cool. In a food processor or blender, or with an immersion blender, purée into a smooth paste. Set aside ¼ cup (60 ml). The leftover chutney can be covered and kept in the refrigerator for at least 1 week.

For the naanzanella
Set a rack inside a baking sheet, line the rack with paper towels, and arrange it near the stove. In a large skillet, heat about 1 inch (2.5 cm) of canola oil over medium-high heat until shimmering. Working in batches, fry the naan, tossing occasionally and lowering the heat as needed, for about 3 minutes or until crispy. Using a slotted spoon, transfer the naan to the paper towel–lined rack to drain and cool. Repeat to fry the remaining naan.

While the naan is cooling, in a small bowl, mix the yogurt with the lemon zest and juice and season to taste with salt.

In a large bowl, toss the naan with ¼ cup (60 ml) of the yogurt mixture, along with ¼ cup (60 ml) each of the mint chutney and tamarind chutney. Add more yogurt and either chutney to taste. Divide the naan mixture among plates, garnish with the strawberries, bhel puri, and edible flowers, if using, and serve.

Lamb Keema Papdi Nachos

Serves 4

The first time I had nachos, the combination of flavors, textures, and colors reminded me of chaat, which are crispy, crunchy, saucy snacks beloved in India. I instantly fell in love, and knew I wanted to create a dish that blended the two together. I included a recipe to make your own *papdi* chips, but you can buy them, along with many of the other ingredients, at Indian markets. The tamarind chutney adds a flavor that almost mimics barbecue sauce.

For the papdi chips
1 cup plus 1 tablespoon (100 g) besan (gram or chickpea flour)
½ teaspoon ajowan seeds
¼ teaspoon black peppercorns, crushed
⅛ teaspoon salt
Baking soda
½ cup (15 g) fresh cilantro leaves, finely chopped
2 teaspoons canola oil, plus more for frying the chips
2 tablespoons all-purpose flour

For the lamb keema
2 tablespoons coconut oil
2 onions, finely chopped
Salt
1 large tomato, finely chopped
½ cup (120 ml) tomato purée
½ tablespoon ginger paste
½ tablespoon garlic paste
2 tablespoons meat masala powder
1 teaspoon chili powder
1 teaspoon dried fenugreek leaves
Granulated sugar
1 pound (450 g) ground lamb
¾ cup (180 ml) water
1 tablespoon chopped fresh cilantro leaves

For the pico de gallo
4 small tomatoes, finely diced
2 small English cucumbers, finely diced
3 small jalapeños (or Fresno chiles), seeded (optional) and finely diced
1 small red onion, finely diced
2 tablespoons freshly squeezed lemon juice
Salt and freshly ground pepper
Chaat masala

For the lemon yogurt
1 cup (240 ml) plain yogurt
3 tablespoons granulated sugar
Zest of 1 lemon
2 tablespoons freshly squeezed lemon juice
Salt

For serving
Tamarind chutney (see page 37), for drizzling
3 ounces (85 g) Provel cheese, grated
½ teaspoon chaat masala, for serving
Pickled jalapeños, for serving

For the papdi chips
In a large bowl, whisk together the besan, ajowan seeds, crushed black peppercorns, salt, and a pinch of baking soda. Stir in the cilantro. Using your hands, rub the canola oil into the mixture then add water, 1 teaspoon at a time, to make a sticky dough. Add the all-purpose flour and knead in the bowl to form a stiff dough.

On a lightly floured work surface, use a rolling pin to roll out the dough until ⅛ inch thick (0.25 cm). Cut the dough into 2-inch (5 cm) pieces.

Set a rack inside a baking sheet and arrange it near the stove. In a large heavy saucepan or Dutch oven, bring about 3 inches (7.5 cm) of canola oil to 350°F (180°C). Working in batches, carefully add a few rounds of dough to the hot oil and fry, occasionally flipping and moving them around in the oil, for about 2 minutes or until crisp and golden yellow. Using a slotted spoon or a strainer with a handle, transfer the chips to the rack to drain and cool. Repeat to fry the remaining chips.

Continued ⟶

Maneet Chauhan

For the lamb keema
In a large skillet, heat the coconut oil over medium-high heat. Add the onions and a pinch of salt and cook, stirring, for about 5 minutes or until lightly browned. Add the tomato and tomato purée and cook for about 5 minutes or until the mixture is thick. Add the ginger and garlic pastes, followed by the meat masala powder and chili powder and cook for about 1 minute or until fragrant. Add the fenugreek leaves, a large pinch of salt, a small pinch of sugar, and the ground lamb and stir to combine. Add the water and bring to a boil. Cook, uncovered, over medium-high heat for about 10 minutes or until most of the liquid evaporates. Season to taste with salt, sprinkle with the cilantro, and keep warm.

For the pico de gallo
In a small bowl, combine the tomatoes, cucumbers, jalapeños, red onion, and lemon juice and season to taste with salt, pepper, and chaat masala. Set aside some of the pico de gallo for serving.

For the lemon yogurt
In a bowl, combine the yogurt, sugar, and the lemon zest and juice and season to taste with salt. Set aside some yogurt for serving. The leftover yogurt can be refrigerated and should be used within 1 or 2 days.

For serving
Set the oven to broil.
Arrange half the papdi chips on an oven-safe platter or baking sheet. Top with half the lamb mixture and a drizzle of tamarind chutney. Add the remaining chips, followed by the remaining lamb mixture and sprinkle with the Provel cheese. Broil a few inches from the heat for 3 to 4 minutes or until the cheese starts to melt.
Top the nachos with some pico de gallo, lemon yogurt, chaat masala, and pickled jalapeños. Serve hot.

"You were born somewhere in the world. It doesn't mean that you don't belong somewhere else. It's very important to know that. When you go somewhere, you make your home. This country belonged to Native Americans. We are all immigrants, in a way. Whether you are in the city or the country—you are with people from all over the world. There is something very special because everyone comes to the table with a different perspective and that allows us each to grow as a person.

I grew up outside Paris, but I surrounded myself with people from Morocco. I wanted to know that culture. It is so rich. We need that, to be able to surround ourselves with "different." Not better, and we're not better either, but they have another story to tell, and that's beautiful and powerful.

You can come to my kitchen today and there are people from Singapore, Ecuador, France, Sweden, Shanghai, America, South Africa, Mexico, Korea, different parts of the world. They all have something that I don't know, and I want to hear their voices. It's important to be curious and share ideas. That's what will make the world better, inclusivity, not exclusivity."

France ⟶ San Francisco, California

Dominique Crenn

Groundbreaking chef Dominique Crenn grew up in France and emigrated in 1988 to start her career at Stars, Jeremiah Tower's fabled restaurant in San Francisco. She has been racking up stars and firsts ever since. In the late 1990s, she became the first female executive chef in Indonesia, when she cooked at the Intercontinental Hotel In Jakarta. In 2018, she became the first female chef in the United States to be awarded three Michelin stars. In 2016, the World's 50 Best Restaurants named her World's Best Female Chef. And in 2018 she won the James Beard Award for Best Chef: West—no "female" modifier needed.

At her restaurant Atelier Crenn (named for her adoptive father, Allain, a politician and artist who took her to fine restaurants and whose paintings are displayed on the walls) and at her two other eateries, Petit Crenn and Bar Crenn, she draws on flavors from her childhood in Versailles and Brittany, while showcasing California ingredients. Crenn has also been featured on the acclaimed popular series *Chef's Table*, and tables at Atelier are booked months ahead. A trained economist with a master's in international business, she likes to say she focuses on "cuisine as a craft and the community as an inspiration."

An active member of the international culinary community, Crenn promotes innovation, sustainability, and equality through panels and summits.

Dominique Crenn

Geoduck Tartelettes

In these tiny tarts, we showcase pristine local ingredients, including sea urchin, geoduck, and citrus. In the winter, we make the rosettes on top of the tarts with thinly sliced citrus segments instead of stone fruit and make the vinegar gel with a mix of citrus juices. This is an ambitious recipe—more for the professional than the home cook—but the techniques and flavor combinations just might inspire you.

Geoduck, a large soft-shell clam native to the Pacific Northwest, can be ordered online. Ultra-Tex 3 is a food starch derived from tapioca and used to create smooth, glossy gels without adding any heat or additional flavor. It's also available online, including from modernistpantry.com.

For the pineapple gel
1 medium pineapple
1 shallot, sliced
2 cloves garlic, smashed
1 jalapeño, roughly chopped
1 stalk lemongrass
    (tender inner bulb only), sliced
Peel of 1 lime
3 cups (720 ml) gooseberry or
    Champagne vinegar
⅓ cup plus 1 tablespoon (90 ml)
    freshly squeezed lime juice
¼ cup (60 ml) shiro dashi
1 (1-inch / 2.5-cm) piece Japanese
    smoke wood stick
1 (¼-ounce / 7-g) envelope
    powdered gelatin

For the mousseline reduction
½ cup (120 ml) gooseberry vinegar
½ cup (120 ml) Champagne vinegar
½ cup (120 ml) white wine
2 shallots, diced
2 tablespoons fresh lemon
    thyme leaves
1½ tablespoons fresh tarragon leaves
Peel of ½ lemon
Peel of ½ lime
1 stalk lemongrass
    (tender inner bulb only), sliced
5 large egg yolks
½ cup (115 g) unsalted butter
1 tablespoon freshly squeezed lemon
    juice, plus more as needed

1 tablespoon shiro dashi,
    plus more as needed
1 teaspoon salt

For the whipped cream
1 cup (240 ml) heavy whipping cream
½ stalk lemongrass
    (white part only), sliced
Zest of 1 lemon
Zest of 1 mandarin orange
Zest of 1 lime
1 teaspoon shiro dashi
¼ teaspoon salt

For the tartelette shells and covers
1¼ cups (143 g) Cup4Cup
    multipurpose gluten-free flour
1 cup (128 g) toasted Koshihikari
    rice flour
6 tablespoons (38 g) brown rice flour
½ cup (100 g) brown sugar
1 tablespoon Maldon salt
¼ tablespoon xanthan gum
¾ cup (170 g) cold unsalted butter,
    cut into small pieces
⅓ (75 ml) cup water
1 large egg

For the vinegar gel
⅔ cup (150 ml) apple cider vinegar
2 teaspoons shiro dashi
1 tablespoon Ultra-Tex 3

For the geoduck
1 (1-pound / 450-g) geoduck

For the browned butter
3 pounds (1.4 kg) unsalted butter
1 tablespoon shiro dashi

For the assembly
1 peach
1 nectarine
1 plum
1 (roughly 4 ½-ounce / 130-g) tray
    shelled fresh uni (sea urchin)

For the pineapple gel
Light a grill or preheat a grill pan over high heat. Using a serrated knife, peel the pineapple and cut it in half lengthwise. Grill the pineapple, turning frequently, for about 5 minutes or until charred on all sides. Transfer to a large bowl, add the shallot, garlic, jalapeño, lemongrass, lime peel, gooseberry vinegar, lime juice, and shiro dashi then cover and refrigerate overnight.

Strain the liquid into a shallow, wide bowl or container that would fit inside a large roasting pan.

Continued ⟶

Dominique Crenn

Place the smoke stick in the roasting pan and set a rack on top. Ignite the stick and when it starts to smoke, arrange the bowl of steeped vinegar on the rack. Cover the pan tightly with foil and allow the liquid to smoke for about 20 minutes. Uncover the pan and remove the bowl. Pour water on the stick so it stops smoking.

Transfer about ¼ cup (60 ml) of the smoked liquid to a small heat-proof bowl and sprinkle with the gelatin. Let stand for about 5 minutes or until the gelatin blooms.

In a medium saucepan, bring the remaining steeped vinegar to a simmer then add the gelatin mixture, whisking until it's dissolved and incorporated.

Strain the mixture into a shallow, preferably metal, container and refrigerate for about 6 hours or until set.

For the mousseline reduction
Fill a large pot with water and heat until the water reaches 167°F (75°C) on a digital probe or candy thermometer.

In a medium saucepan, combine the gooseberry and Champagne vinegars, the white wine, shallots, lemon thyme, tarragon, lemon and lime peels, and lemongrass and bring to a boil over high heat. Continue boiling for about 10 minutes or until reduced by two-thirds.

Strain the mixture into a vacuum-pack or a medium BPA-free resealable freezer bag. Add the egg yolks and butter and vacuum seal the bag. If using a freezer bag, seal all but 1 corner and gradually lower the bag into a large bowl of water until nearly all of the air is pressed out, then seal.

Add the bag to the pot of 167°F (75°C) water and cook, maintaining the temperature, for 30 minutes. Remove the bag and transfer the contents to a high-speed blender.

Add the lemon juice, shiro dashi, and salt and purée until smooth. Taste and season with more lemon juice, shiro dashi, and salt as needed. Refrigerate until ready to use.

For the whipped cream
In a vacuum-pack or medium BPA-free resealable freezer bag, combine the heavy whipping cream, lemongrass, the lemon, mandarin orange, and lime zest, the shiro dashi, and salt. Vacuum seal the bag. If using a freezer bag, seal all but 1 corner and gradually lower the bag into a large bowl of water until nearly all of the air is pressed out, then seal. Refrigerate overnight.

For the tartelette shells and covers
In a food processor, pulse together the gluten-free, rice, and brown rice flours, the brown sugar, Maldon salt, xanthan gum, and butter until the butter is the size of small peas. Transfer to a bowl and add the water and egg. Using your hands, mix until incorporated.

Separate the dough so you have a piece that's about ⅓ of the total and another piece that's about ⅔ of the total.

Preheat the oven to 375°F (190°C). Line 2 baking sheets with silicone liners or parchment paper.

Using a pasta machine, roll out the smaller piece of dough until you reach Setting 4. Arrange the sheet of dough on a lightly floured work surface. Using a round 1½-inch (4 cm) cutter, stamp out 50 to 60 rounds and transfer to the prepared baking sheets, leaving about 1 inch (2.5 cm) between each round. Bake, turning once halfway through, for about 15 minutes or until golden brown. Repeat until all the rounds have been baked. Let cool completely. These are the tartelette covers.

While the covers are baking, using the pasta machine, roll out the larger piece of dough until you reach Setting 5. Arrange the sheet of dough on a lightly floured work surface. Using a round 3-inch (7.5 cm) cutter, stamp out 50 to 60 rounds. Press the rounds into 1¾-inch (4.5 cm) unfluted tartelette molds. Trim any edges. These are the tartelette shells. Transfer the shells to baking sheets and bake, turning once halfway through, for about 15 minutes or until golden brown. Let cool completely, then unmold. The tartelette shells and covers can be stored in airtight containers overnight.

For the vinegar gel
In a bowl, whisk together the apple cider vinegar and shiro dashi. Gradually add the Ultra-Tex, whisking constantly, until it reaches the consistency of toothpaste. This will act as a glue for the garnishes.

For the geoduck
Fill a large bowl with ice water and bring a large saucepan of water to a boil.

Reduce the water to a simmer and using tongs, dunk the whole geoduck in the water for 10 seconds to loosen the skin and the shell, then transfer to the ice water. Once cool, use your hands to remove the brown outer skin from the siphon (the part that hangs outside the shell). Carefully cut along both sides of the shell, and using your hands, pry open the shell. Cut the clam from the shell and pull off and discard the stomach and other innards. Rinse the siphon and clam belly (the meaty part from inside the shell). Separate the siphon from the belly and reserve the belly for another use, such as fritters. Cut off and discard the dark tip from the siphon, if desired. Cover and refrigerate the geoduck siphon, preferably on a bed of ice, until you are ready to use, up to 2 hours.

For the browned butter
In a medium saucepan, cook the butter over medium-low heat without stirring until the golden fat is separated from the milk solids. When the butter is translucent, increase the heat to medium and cook until the solids on the bottom of the pot toast and the butter smells nutty. Strain through a coffee filter into a clean saucepan. Add the shiro dashi and keep warm.

For the assembly
Cut ⅓-inch-thick (7.5 mm) slices from the rounded edges of the peach, nectarine, and plum. Shave these pieces lengthwise into very thin slices and reserve to make rosettes.

Cut the remaining fruit into ¼-inch (0.5 cm) dice.

Set the clarified browned butter over low to medium-low heat and bring to 167°F (75°C). Add the diced fruit and poach for 30 minutes. Using a slotted spoon, transfer the fruit to a bowl. Add the uni to the butter and poach for about 15 minutes. Using a slotted spoon, transfer the uni to a cutting board and cut into 50 to 60 pieces to match the number of shells you have.

Holding a sharp knife at an angle, very thinly slice the geoduck siphon crosswise.

Arrange the tartelette shells on a work surface. Scoop a small spoonful of pineapple gel into each shell. Spoon a little bit of the poached fruit on top followed by a piece of poached uni. Set the round pastry discs on top, pressing to make them flush with the shells if necessary. Working in an alternating pattern, use the thinly sliced geoduck and thinly sliced fruit to form rosettes on top of each tartelette, gluing the pieces together with the vinegar gel.

Strain the steeped heavy whipping cream into a large bowl, and using an electric mixer, whip to stiff peaks. Fold the whipped cream into the mousseline reduction.

Arrange the tartelettes on plates, dollop with the mousseline, and serve.

Vietnam ⟶ Chicago, Illinois

Thai Dang

When Thai Dang was a child, he moved with his parents and eight siblings from Vietnam to the Washington, DC area. Stateside, he grew up on traditional Vietnamese dishes like crispy noodles with peppers and green papaya salad with fermented shrimp.

Dang's passion for the culinary world and family values stem from the kitchen table, where as a boy he built relationships through food. This pushed him to enroll at L'Academie de Cuisine in Maryland where he mastered French techniques, after which he spent years honing his craft at the award-winning CityZen, a AAA Four-Diamond at the Mandarin Oriental in Washington, DC; at the three-Michelin-starred L2o; and as Chef de Cuisine of RIA restaurant at the Elysian Hotel (now Waldorf Astoria Chicago), where he helped guide the team to two Michelin stars by focusing on fresh flavors coupled with his contemporary approach to technique and presentation.

Dang and his wife Danielle now run HaiSous, showcasing the depth of Vietnamese flavors in the heart of Chicago. HaiSous was nominated as a semifinalist for the Best New Restaurant award by the James Beard Foundation in 2018 and was awarded a Bib Gourmand by Michelin. Dang was twice nominated as *Food & Wine* People's Choice Chef of the Year.

"Cooking has always been a way for me to preserve my culture and express it to a world less familiar with those flavors or to delight those who already understand Vietnamese cuisine. It gives me joy to introduce Vietnamese ingredients and inspire the staff and guests with my flavors and style of cooking. There is a special place for immigrants in my kitchen. We understand the struggle of adapting to a new homeland. I couldn't be more proud to be able to represent Vietnamese cuisine in my own way here in America."

Thai Dang

Shrimp with Sweet Onions and Vietnamese Coriander

Serves 6 to 8

Vietnamese cuisine is famous for shrimp dishes and an abundant use of fresh herbs, and this recipe features both.

2½ pounds (1.1 kg) colossal (8/12 count) shrimp, peeled and deveined
1¾ cups (210 g) cornstarch
1½ cups (210 g) rice flour
Salt and freshly ground pepper
Canola oil
2 Vidalia or other large sweet onions, halved and cut into ¼-inch-thick (0.5 cm) slices
3 large cloves garlic, minced
1 teaspoon fish sauce plus ½ cup (120 ml) for serving
½ teaspoon granulated sugar
1 large handful chopped fresh Vietnamese coriander (rau răm) or regular cilantro, washed in ice water, drained, and dried
1 fresh Thai chile, thinly sliced
Steamed rice, for serving

Split the shrimp down the center so they are not completely butterflied but will fan out slightly when cooked.

In a large bowl, whisk together the cornstarch and rice flour and season to taste with salt and pepper. Set a rack inside a baking sheet and arrange it near the stove. In a large, deep skillet, heat ¼ to ½ inch (0.5 to 1.25 cm) of canola oil over medium-high heat until shimmering. Working in batches, add the shrimp to the cornstarch mixture, toss, and tap off any excess. Add a single layer of shrimp to the hot oil and fry, turning and adjusting the heat as needed, for about 30 seconds or until they start to turn golden but are not cooked through. Transfer to the rack and continue frying shrimp, adding more oil between batches as needed. When you're done frying the shrimp, drain off the oil.

In the same skillet, heat 3 tablespoons of canola oil over medium heat. Add the sweet onions and cook, stirring, for about 4 minutes or until starting to soften. Add the garlic and cook for about 1 minute or until fragrant. Add 1 teaspoon of the fish sauce and the sugar and season to taste with salt and pepper. When the onions are tender, add the shrimp and Vietnamese coriander and cook for 2 to 4 minutes or until the shrimp are cooked through.

Divide the remaining ½ cup (120 ml) of fish sauce between 2 small bowls and add some Thai chile to each.

Transfer the shrimp to plates and serve with steamed rice and the Thai chile dipping sauce.

Thai Dang

Grilled Salmon and Snow Fungus Salad with Vietnamese Herbs (Gọi cá)

Serves 4 to 6

Snow fungus is a gelatinous mushroom prized for its texture and renowned healing properties. Often used in desserts or drinks, here it's served in a salad with traditional Vietnamese herbs. Find the herbs at Vietnamese or Chinese markets (where you can also find the snow fungus in dried form), or simply substitute Thai basil and regular cilantro. Keep herbs fresh in an ice water bath then spin dry and drain on paper towels.

For the snow fungus and salmon
¼ pound (110 g) dried snow fungus
Canola oil
1 (2-pound / 900-g) skin-on or
    skinless salmon fillet

For the pickled cucumber
¼ cup (60 ml) rice vinegar
1 tablespoon granulated sugar
Salt
1 English cucumber, thinly sliced

For the ginger nuoc cham
4 teaspoons granulated sugar
¼ cup (60 ml) water, warm
3 tablespoons freshly squeezed
    lime juice
2 to 3 fresh Thai chiles, thinly
    sliced
2 tablespoons minced fresh ginger
2 cloves garlic, minced
⅓ cup (75 ml) fish sauce
1 teaspoon rice vinegar

For serving
½ large white onion, thinly sliced
1 large handful mixed fresh
    Vietnamese herbs, such as *tía
    tô* (shiso) *rau răm* (Vietnamese
    coriander), *huế* (Thai basil), and
    kinh giới (lemon balm), washed
    in ice water, drained, and dried
Fresh dill fronds (optional)

For the snow fungus and salmon
Set the snow fungus in a large bowl and bring a kettle of water to a boil. Cover the snow fungus with the boiling water and let stand until the water is completely cool and the snow fungus is soft. Drain and break or slice the fungus into bite-size pieces.

Light a grill and heat to medium high. Very lightly oil the grill grates with canola oil if needed to prevent sticking. Add the salmon, skin-side down if skin-on, cover, and grill for 5 to 8 minutes or until a knife inserted in the thickest part feels warm to the touch for medium rare and hot for more well done. Transfer to a cutting board or platter and let cool completely.

For the pickled cucumber
In a medium bowl, whisk together the rice vinegar and sugar then balance the flavors with a pinch of salt. Add the cucumber, toss, and let stand for 10 minutes then drain.

For the ginger nuoc cham
In a medium bowl, whisk the sugar and warm water until the sugar is dissolved. Add the lime juice, Thai chiles, ginger, and garlic, and stir. Add the fish sauce and rice vinegar, taste, and add more of each if needed to balance the flavors.

For serving
In a large bowl, toss the snow fungus and sliced white onion with about 2 tablespoons of the ginger nuoc cham. Add about ¾ of the mixed fresh herbs. Tear the cooled salmon into large chunks, discarding any skin, and add to the bowl. Gently toss the salad, being sure not to overmix it or break up the salmon pieces too much. Taste and add more of the ginger nuoc cham, if desired. Transfer the salad to bowls, top with the pickled cucumber, more herbs, and the dill fronds, if using. Serve with more ginger nuoc cham alongside.

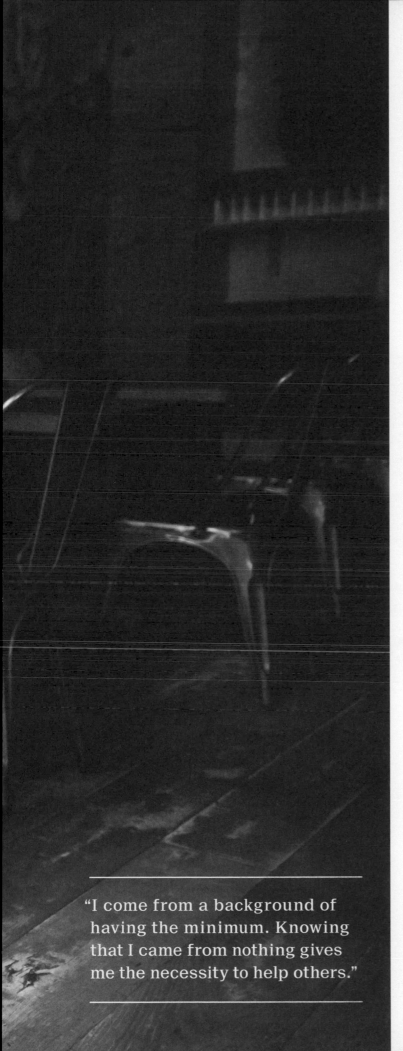

Peru ⟶ Washington, DC

Carlos Delgado

Growing up in Peru, Carlos Delgado learned how to kill chickens and butcher fish before the age of six. Today he is head chef at José Andrés's China Chilcano in Washington, DC, and calls himself "a Peruvian ambassador," one who imports a special type of chocolate and has plans to bring in pisco, too.

The path wasn't easy. Delgado immigrated to live with his mother when he was twelve years old, not knowing English but hoping to become a chef, then had a child at sixteen and had to drop out of school. After getting his GED in exactly one month, he was running both the kitchen and dining room at a small family restaurant; soon he was cooking for renowned chef Brian Voltaggio at Volt, where the young Delgado showed serious talents. He attended culinary school and traveled back and forth to Peru to further study his homeland's cuisine, then opened his own restaurant, Ocopa, which landed on *Washingtonian* magazine's 100 Very Best Restaurants list and also got Michelin's notice.

In 2015, Delgado went to work for Chef José Andrés. As head chef at China Chilcano, Delgado blends Chinese and Japanese influences with those Peruvian flavors he's been mastering since childhood.

"I come from a background of having the minimum. Knowing that I came from nothing gives me the necessity to help others."

Carlos Delgado

Ceviche Nikkei

Nikkei is the name of the fusion cuisine that emerged after workers emigrated from Japan to Peru in the 19th century. In this version of ceviche, you'll find soy sauce, sake, and furikake seasoning. The light soy sauce in the ponzu sauce has a lighter color and thinner texture but is saltier than regular soy sauce; using the two together helps balance the flavor nicely. To bring the recipe together more quickly, you can substitute store-bought ponzu sauce. Since it's usually made with lemon juice, just add a squeeze of lime.

For the cured eggs
¾ cup (180 ml) regular soy sauce
¼ cup (60 ml) sake
1 bunch scallions (white parts only), thinly sliced
8 fresh large egg yolks

For the ponzu sauce
2 cups plus 1 tablespoon (495 ml) light soy sauce
¾ cup plus 2 tablespoons (210 ml) freshly squeezed lime juice
½ cup (120 ml) rice vinegar
½ cup (120 ml) fish stock
½ cup (120 ml) regular soy sauce
1 (½-ounce / 15 g) piece kombu

For the ceviche
1½ pounds (680 g) fresh sushi-grade tuna, preferably top loin, cut into 1-inch (2.5 cm) pieces
2 jicamas, peeled and cut into small cubes
2 ripe avocadoes, peeled and cut into small cubes
4 red onions, very thinly sliced on a mandoline
1 bunch scallions (green parts only), cut into matchsticks
Furikake, for serving

For the cured eggs
In a small saucepan, bring the regular soy sauce, sake, and scallions to a boil. Continue boiling for about 4 minutes or until the alcohol cooks off. Remove from the heat and let cool completely. Gently add the egg yolks, cover, and refrigerate for 2 to 6 hours.

For the ponzu sauce
In a large bowl, whisk together the light soy sauce, lime juice, rice vinegar, fish stock, and regular soy sauce then add the kombu and let soak for at least 5 minutes. Remove the kombu before using. (To make the ponzu sauce ahead, wait to add the lime juice, cover, and refrigerate overnight then add the lime juice just before using.)

For the ceviche
Divide the tuna among 8 chilled shallow bowls and top each with about 5 pieces of the jicama. Arrange the avocado around the tuna.

Pour ¼ cup (60 ml) of the ponzu sauce into each bowl and set a cured egg yolk in the middle of each. Garnish with little piles of wispy red onions and scallions. Generously sprinkle furikake over half of each egg yolk to create a half moon design and serve immediately.

Carlos Delgado

Pegao Norteño

This is a magical dish. You make a cumin crêpe batter and cook lamb dumplings atop it. As the liquid reduces, the dumplings are set into a crisp, lacey crêpe, then you flip the whole thing over to serve. At the restaurant, I garnish the crêpe with gold leaf but the recipe is adapted here for home use.

For the dough
4¼ cups (550 g) all-purpose flour
2 teaspoons salt
1¼ cups (300 ml) water

For the filling
1 ounce (28 g) fresh cilantro
½ cup (120 ml) canola oil
½ pound (225 g) seeded kabocha squash, flesh finely grated
2 white onions, finely diced
6 ounces (170 g) ají amarillo paste
½ head garlic, minced
1 pound (450 g) ground lamb
1 bunch scallions, thinly sliced
3 ounces (85 g) fresh ginger, minced
1 teaspoon ground cumin
¼ cup (60 ml) chicken stock
⅓ cup plus 1 tablespoon (90 ml) aged soy sauce
½ teaspoon salt

For the cumin lace
¼ cup (30 g) all-purpose flour
¼ cup (30 g) cornstarch
1 teaspoon salt
½ teaspoon ground cumin
2 cups (480 ml) water

For serving
2 cups (480 ml) canola oil

For the dough
In the bowl of a stand mixer fitted with the dough hook attachment, combine the flour and salt with the water and mix with the hook until a smooth dough forms—the dough should have a clean sheen and no longer be sticky. If the dough seems too dry, add a little more water, 1 teaspoon at a time. Cover with plastic wrap and let rest for 1 hour at room temperature.

Divide the dough into 2 equal pieces. Using a pasta maker, roll 1 piece of dough at a time until as thin as a penny. Repeat with the other piece of dough. Using a 3-inch (7.5 cm) round cookie cutter, cut the dough into about 56 rounds. (If stacking the rounds, dust them well with flour so they don't stick to each other; do not reroll the scraps; instead, cut them into free-form noodles and boil separately.)

For the filling
In a mini food processor, process the cilantro until puréed.

In a large skillet, heat the canola oil over medium heat. Add the kabocha squash, white onions, ají amarillo paste, and garlic and cook over low heat, stirring frequently to avoid burning, for about 45 minutes or until the flavors meld and the vegetables are very tender. Remove from the heat, transfer to a food processor, and purée until smooth.

In a large bowl, combine the ground lamb, scallions, ginger, and cumin and mix well. Gradually add the chicken stock and the puréed squash mixture and mix until incorporated. Fold in the aged soy sauce,

salt, and the puréed cilantro—the mixture should be wet, smooth, and consistent.

Working with 1 round of dough at a time, set 1 tablespoon of the filling in the center. Using your thumbs, fold the round of dough over to enclose the filling and form a half moon shape, pressing tightly to seal. Repeat with the remaining filling and rounds of dough to make more dumplings.

For the cumin lace
In a small bowl, combine the flour, cornstarch, salt, and cumin with the water.

For serving
In a large nonstick skillet with a tight-fitting lid, heat ¼ cup (60 ml) of the canola oil over medium-high heat until shimmering. Stir the cumin lace to make sure it's blended then add ¼ cup (60 ml) to the pan. Cook until reduced by half then arrange 7 dumplings on top of the lace. Cover the skillet with the lid, reduce the heat to low, and steam the dumplings as the cumin lace continues to reduce. Remove the lid and make sure the underside of the lace is evenly crispy, adjusting the position of the pan to make sure it's cooking evenly. Cover the pan with the lid again and carefully flip the pan so the lace detaches from the pan. Slide the dumplings and lace onto a plate and keep hot. Repeat with the remaining oil, cumin lace, and dumplings and serve hot.

Quebec, Canada ⟶ Queens, New York

Hugue Dufour

Swagger might not be considered a Quebecois trait, but Hugue Dufour carries it off with Queens-style flair. Growing up in Alma, Lac St. Jean, Quebec, surrounded by cabbage fields and dairy cows, he was steeped in traditional regional flavors, which he'd eventually reimagine in over-the-top interpretations. He left his small town to briefly attend cooking school in Montreal before working his way through serious kitchens like Toqué! and the carnivores' cult favorite, Au Pied de Cochon. As a partner in the latter, he gained acclaim through a documentary, a cookbook album and a television show. After immigrating to the United States to join his partner Sarah Obraitis in New York City, the two opened the groundbreaking, genre-defying M. Wells in a Long Island City diner in 2010, serving Dufour's interpretations of French-Canadian recipes ramped up with American excess.

When the diner's extraordinary fame and media frenzy caused its rent to skyrocket, Dufour packed his knives and opened M. Wells Dinette, which operated in MoMA PS1 until early 2019, and M. Wells Steakhouse in a former auto body shop. Michelin gives the steakhouse two forks of approval for its unique, outsized flavors.

"As a newcomer to the States—and I always feel like one—I have to (and want to) work harder, produce super creatively, and provide evermore. My hope is that my family, friends, guests, and the community at large benefit in lasting ways from my extra effort."

Hugue Dufour

Coquilles St. Hugues

Serves 4

Herbes salées, which translates to "salted herbs," is a classic Quebecois condiment made of ingredients from the garden at the end of the year: Finely chopped celery, onions, carrots, parsnips, parsley, chervil, winter savory, leeks, chives, and spinach are mixed with coarse sea salt and can be preserved all year long. The result is a wonderful seasoning for soups and stews. Scallop shells can be purchased online, but you can also use small ramekins or other small baking dishes.

For the herbes salées
1 medium leek, cleaned and
    roughly chopped
1 medium carrot, roughly chopped
1 celery stalk, roughly chopped
1 small parsnip, roughly chopped
½ medium white onion, roughly
    chopped
1 cup (30 g) roughly chopped
    spinach
1 cup (30 g) fresh flat-leaf parsley
1 cup (45 g) roughly chopped
    fresh chives
⅓ cup (100 g) coarse sea salt

For the coquilles
1½ cups (340 g) unsalted butter
1 onion, finely diced
1 carrot, finely diced
1 celery stalk, finely diced
5 ounces (140 g) small button
    mushrooms, quartered
¼ cup (30 g) all-purpose flour
½ cup (120 ml) white wine
1½ cups (360 ml) heavy cream
¼ pound (110 g) bay scallops
¼ pound (110 g) small shrimp,
    such as Maine shrimp, peeled
    and deveined
1 dozen littleneck clams,
    steamed open*
1 cooked lobster tail, diced
2 ounces (60 g) smoked sturgeon
    fillet, cubed
½ cup (55 g) sea beans
    (sea asparagus)
Freshly ground pepper
4 Yukon gold potatoes, peeled
Salt

2 large egg yolks
4 (6-inch / 15-cm) scallop shells
½ pound (225 g) Gruyère, grated
Sweet paprika, for dusting

*To steam clams open, bring ¼ cup of water to a boil in a saucepan. Add the clams, cover, and steam just until the clams open. Remove the meat and discard the shells.

For the herbes salées
In a food processor, combine the leek, carrot, celery, parsnip, and onion and pulse until finely chopped. Add the spinach, parsley, and chives and pulse until even more finely chopped. Transfer to a jar with a lid, add the salt, and stir to combine. Cover and refrigerate overnight. Set aside 1 tablespoon of the herbes salées. The leftover amount will keep, in an airtight jar in the refrigerator, for up to 1 month.

For the coquilles
In a saucepan, melt ½ cup (115 g) of the butter over medium heat. Add the onion, carrot, celery, and mushrooms and cook for about 8 minutes or until softened but not at all browned. Stir in the flour and cook for 2 minutes. Add the white wine and 1 cup (240 ml) of the heavy cream. The mixture will be thick. Stir in the bay scallops, shrimp, littleneck clams, lobster tail, and

smoked sturgeon and cook for about 4 minutes. Remove from the heat, add the sea beans and 1 tablespoon of herbes salées, and season to taste with pepper.

In a medium saucepan, cover the potatoes with cold water and bring to a boil. Lower the heat and simmer for about 20 minutes or until tender then drain. Press the potatoes through a fine-mesh sieve into a bowl then return the potatoes to the saucepan and add the remaining ½ cup (120 ml) of heavy cream. Cook over low heat and when the purée is hot, whisk in the remaining 1 cup (225 g) of butter. Season to taste with salt and pepper and let cool slightly then stir in the egg yolks. Spoon the potatoes into a piping bag fitted with a star tip.

Preheat the oven to 400°F (200°C).

Pipe the potatoes around the rim of each scallop shell to create a barrier then spoon enough of the seafood mixture into the shells to be level with the potatoes. Cover the seafood mixture with a handful of grated Gruyère cheese and bake for 10 to 15 minutes or until the cheese is gratinéed. Dust with paprika and serve.

Hugue Dufour

Pickled Pork Tongue

This dish was on the M. Wells menu from the beginning. When it debuted, the *New Yorker* described it as "smoky and craveable as the best carnitas."

8 pork tongues
2 sprigs fresh rosemary
2 sprigs fresh thyme
1 teaspoon black peppercorns
1 teaspoon juniper berries
2 cups (480 ml) distilled white
    vinegar
1 cup (240 ml) water
½ cup kosher salt
1 cup (200 g) pearl onions, peeled
Unsalted butter
Dijon mustard
Saltines

In a large saucepan, cover the tongues with cold water and bring to a boil. Lower the heat and simmer for about 3 hours or until the tongues are tender. Remove the tongues from the water and let cool then remove and discard the outer skins. Cut the tongues in half lengthwise. Stack the pieces in a 1-quart (960 ml) jar. Tuck in the rosemary, thyme, black peppercorns, and juniper berries.

In a small pot, bring the distilled white vinegar, water, kosher salt, and pearl onions to a boil. Lower the heat and simmer for 5 minutes. Pour the pearl onions and pickling liquid over the tongues then seal the jar and refrigerate for at least 24 hours.

In a skillet, melt ½ teaspoon of butter over medium heat. Working in batches, add a few pieces of tongue and cook gently for about 3 minutes or just until warm. Repeat to cook the remaining tongue, adding more butter as needed. Serve the pickled tongue with Dijon mustard and saltines.

Diego Galicia

"My main mission in the restaurant is to let people know that Mexican food can be elevated, it doesn't have to be cheap or fast. It's important to promote that, especially during these political times. The US is a fertile land for brilliant people from all over the world to come and succeed."

Diego Galicia moved to the US to attend the University of Texas, San Antonio, but quickly took up the study of cooking instead. Determined to become the best at his craft, he enrolled at the Culinary Institute of America's just-opened San Antonio campus through a scholarship for Hispanic students named El Sueño, or The Dream.

Upon graduation, he cooked at Michelin-starred restaurants including Atelier Crenn in San Francisco and Moto in Chicago, but his dream was to showcase the diversity and history of his native Mexican cuisine with serious, precise, and modern preparations.

Back in Texas, he and a business partner scraped together just $15,000 and found an empty train car that was available for $700 a month. "I said, 'Perfect!'" Galicia recalls. On Mixtli's opening night, in 2013, Chef Rick Bayless came in for dinner. Rave reviews hailed Mixtli as the top new restaurant in San Antonio, and national media took notice, too, with *Food & Wine* hailing Galicia as one of the year's Best New Chefs in the country. Things haven't slowed down since.

Today Mixtli draws diners from across the country, its prix-fixe menu changing every forty-five days to showcase a different Mexican region or style. Foods like Oaxacan chocolate with a traditional cloud print, house-nixtamalized corn, or a Mayan dish of quinoa, roe, and avocado, are paired with fables and folklore. Mixtli is now regarded as San Antonio's best restaurant and Galicia has been named a semifinalist for the Best Chef: Southwest award by the James Beard Foundation.

Diego Galicia

Vanilla-Cured Duck Breasts with Butter and Apple

Serves 4

People go to Bath & Body Works and come out thinking vanilla is French. I'm here to remind people that vanilla is native to Mexico! These are the kinds of ideas that I try to push forward, one dinner at a time. That Mexico isn't what you see on your television: It's a huge, diverse, beautiful, inclusive country. And I start with things like vanilla. In this recipe, I use it to cure duck, which I serve with apples from Chihuahua, home to some of the world's best orchards.

For the duck breasts
2 large duck breasts,
    about 14 ounces (400 g) each
1 vanilla bean
Salt

For the pickled apple
2½ cups (600 ml) distilled white
    vinegar
1 cup (240 ml) water
2 cups (400 g) granulated sugar
½ cup (110 g) fine salt
½ cup (60 g) pickling spice mix
    (mustard seeds, coriander,
    cinnamon sticks, celery seeds,
    and black peppercorns)
1 large Honeycrisp apple,
    cut into thin wedges

For the sauce
2 cups (480 ml) apple juice
¼ cup (60 ml) apple cider vinegar
½ cup (115 g) unsalted butter,
    cut into cubes and cold
1 cup (240 ml) heavy cream
Juice of ½ large lemon
Salt

For serving
Mixed greens or pea tendrils

For the duck breasts
Pat the duck breasts dry. Using a sharp knife, score the skin in a cross-hatch pattern to help render the fat and crisp the skin when searing. Flip the duck breasts so they are fat-side down. Split the vanilla bean and scrape out the seeds then rub the seeds into the non-fat sides of the duck breasts and season to taste with salt. Vacuum pack the duck breasts in a medium-sized bag and set a water bath to 144°F (62°C). Place the vacuum-packed duck breasts in the water bath and cook for 1 hour and 30 minutes. Remove the duck breasts from the water bath and set on a sheet pan then top with 2 additional sheet pans and a heavy weight, such as a cast-iron pan, and refrigerate for 6 to 8 hours.

For the pickled apple
In a saucepan, bring the distilled white vinegar, water, sugar, and salt to a boil, stirring to dissolve the sugar and salt. Remove from the heat, add the pickling spice mix, and let cool.
    Put the apple wedges in a vacuum-pack or resealable bag and add 1 cup (240 ml) of the pickling liquid. (Use the remaining pickling liquid to pickle some vegetables!) Vacuum seal the bag or close the bag and squeeze out any excess air. Refrigerate for 6 to 8 hours.

For the sauce
In a medium saucepan, bring the apple juice and apple cider vinegar to a boil. Continue boiling until reduced by a third. Gradually add the cubed butter, whisking constantly to incorporate, then add the heavy cream and lemon juice and whisk until fully blended. Season to taste with salt.

For serving
Remove the duck breasts from the bag and pat them dry. Heat a heavy-bottomed skillet over medium-high heat then add the duck, fat-side down, and sear, turning occasionally, for about 5 minutes or until the meat is warmed through and the skin is crisp. Halve the duck breasts and divide among plates. Arrange some pickled apple wedges alongside and spoon some sauce on the plates. Top with mixed greens or pea tendrils and serve.

Diego Galicia

Smoked Honey Yogurt with Whey Snow and White Grape Syrup

I always love the look of a white dessert. In developing this dish, we focused on a beautiful area of the Trans-Mexican Volcanic Belt. The snow-capped peaks in this mountainous region are breathtakingly beautiful, so I thought, let's do a dessert inspired by them. It uses frozen whey and the flavor is just perfect—a little sweet, a little tangy, and completely balanced.

You can buy smoked honey or simply stir a little smoked paprika into honey. The yield varies depending on what size portions you want to serve.

1 quart (960 ml) full-fat plain
　Greek yogurt
2 cups (480 ml) simple syrup*,
　plus more to taste
2 cups (480 ml) smoked honey
2 cups (480 ml) high quality white
　grape juice or freshly pressed
　grape juice
Cheesecloth

To make simple syrup, combine equal parts water and granulated sugar in a saucepan and bring to a boil, stirring to dissolve the sugar. Let cool and store in the refrigerator.

Line a large colander with 2 layers of cheesecloth and set it in a bowl that will hold the colander at least 2 inches (5 cm) above the bottom of the bowl. Scoop the yogurt into the lined colander, cover, and place in the refrigerator to strain for about 8 hours or overnight. (Alternatively, you can tie the cheesecloth at the top with kitchen string and hang the yogurt over a bowl to catch the whey.)

Reserve the whey and sweeten to taste with simple syrup. Pour the sweetened whey into a rimmed baking sheet or freezer-safe baking dish, cover, and freeze overnight.

In a large bowl, use a rubber spatula to combine the strained yogurt and smoked honey. Pour the mixture into an ice cream machine and freeze according to the manufacturer's instructions until semisoft. Transfer to a freezer-safe, airtight container and freeze overnight.

In a large bowl, whisk the white grape juice with simple syrup to taste. (If using freshly pressed juice, strain it through a coffee filter or paper towel to remove any impurities first.) Transfer to a pitcher.

When ready to serve, let the frozen yogurt stand at room temperature for 5 to 10 minutes or until soft enough to scoop. Scrape the whey with a fork to create a snow-like powder and arrange small piles in bowls. Use 2 spoons to form the frozen yogurt into quenelle shapes, if desired, and set one or more in each bowl. Serve with the grape syrup alongside.

Colombia ⟶ New York, New York

Cesar Gutierrez

Cesar Gutierrez remembers starving as a four-year-old fleeing Colombia in 1994, when he and his mother and twin brother set out through Mexico for the United States. Today he is sous chef at Daniel Boulud's Café Boulud in New York City, which boasts two Michelin stars. The road in between was rocky: As a teen, he dropped out of high school and worked at a Burger King. But he found his footing, got his GED, moved on to a Manhattan technical school, and won a scholarship to the world-renowned French Culinary Institute (now the International Culinary Center). He credits the Careers through Culinary Arts Program with setting him on the path to success by placing him at BLT Prime, as well as Chef Boulud's involvement with the Institut Paul Bocuse in Lyon, France.

Despite becoming sous chef at one of the country's top restaurants, Gutierrez isn't resting on his laurels: he dreams of opening his own restaurant, with a farm or garden attached, and also of representing his adopted country in the Bocuse d'Or, the most competitive cooking contest for chefs. In the meantime, he isn't only cooking French food. His childhood-inspired Colombian dishes have been featured on Café Boulud's famous "Le Voyage" menus.

"Like many immigrants, my parents wanted to give their children the opportunities that they did not have. I have always tried to bring my culture into the kitchen, whether it be making empanadas for staff meal or making a full Colombian menu at Café Boulud that ran for four months. I was proud to present this menu at a Michelin-starred French restaurant."

Cesar Gutierrez

Scallops with Ponzu-Poached Butternut Squash

Serves 4

The recipe makes more lovage aïoli and butternut squash purée than needed, but both can be used in other dishes. Celtuce is a type of lettuce (also called stem lettuce or Chinese lettuce) that's grown not for its leaves but for its succulent center stalk. It has a slightly nutty flavor and can be found at Asian markets. The ponzu must be made at least one week ahead so plan accordingly!

For the ponzu
(or use store-bought ponzu)
1½ ounces (45 g) katsuobushi
    (bonito flakes)
1 (4-inch / 10-cm) piece kombu
1 cup plus 1 tablespoon
    (255 ml) soy sauce
⅔ cup (150 ml) rice vinegar
¼ cup plus 3 tablespoons
    (105 ml) yuzu juice
¼ cup plus 3 tablespoons
    (105 ml) Akasake mirin
Cheesecloth

For the lovage aïoli
½ pound (225 g) lovage leaves
    (or celery leaves)
1 cup (240 ml) extra-virgin olive oil
1 cup (240 ml) canola oil
3 large egg whites
Salt

For the butternut squash purée
3 tablespoons unsalted butter
4 medium shallots, thinly sliced
1 whole butternut squash, peeled
    and cut into 1-inch (2.5 cm)
    cubes
1 cup (240 ml) heavy cream
Salt

For the butternut squash discs
1 butternut squash neck, peeled

For the assembly
1 celtuce, peeled and cut into
    4-inch (10 cm) julienne
1 butternut squash neck, peeled
    and cut into 4-inch (10 cm)
    julienne
8 large sea scallops, thinly sliced
    into rounds
20 small marigold flowers

For the ponzu
In a glass jar or nonreactive container, combine the katsuobushi and kombu. Add the soy sauce, rice vinegar, yuzu juice, and Akasake mirin and stir to gently submerge the katsuobushi and kombu. Cover the container with a tight fitting lid and refrigerate for 1 to 2 weeks before using.

Drain the ponzu through lightly moistened cheesecloth and discard the kombu and katsuobushi. The strained ponzu can be refrigerated in a sanitized jar for up to 1 week.

For the lovage aïoli
In a blender, purée the lovage leaves with the extra-virgin olive oil and canola oil until bright green and smooth. Strain the oil through a coffee filter or paper towel into a jar or small pitcher. Clean out and dry the blender.

Put the egg whites in a clean, dry blender and start the motor. With the motor running, gradually drizzle in the lovage oil to create a mayonnaise-like texture. Season to taste with salt. Cover and refrigerate until ready to use or for up to 2 days.

Continued ⟶

Cesar Gutierrez

For the butternut squash purée
Preheat the oven to 350°F (180°C).

In a large ovenproof skillet, melt the butter over medium heat. Add the shallots and cook, stirring occasionally, for 2 to 3 minutes or until tender but not browned. Add the butternut squash cubes, stir to coat with the butter and shallots, and cook just until the squash starts to release water.

Cover the pan tightly with an oven-proof lid or foil and bake for about 45 minutes or until the squash is tender. Transfer to a blender or food processor, add the heavy cream, and purée until smooth. Season to taste with salt. Cover and refrigerate until ready to use or for up to 2 days.

For the butternut squash discs
Thinly slice the butternut squash neck crosswise then use a ring or biscuit cutter to punch out discs that are about the same size as the scallops (1½ to 2 inches / 4 to 5 cm).

In a deep, wide skillet, bring the ponzu to a bare simmer over medium heat. Add the butternut squash discs and poach for 8 to 10 minutes or until just barely tender. Drain the butternut squash discs and refrigerate for at least 1 hour or until well chilled.

For the assembly
Put the lovage aïoli and butternut squash purée into separate piping bags fitted with fine tips. In the center of each of 4 chilled plates or shallow bowls, arrange the celtuce and butternut squash julienne in a small pile, reserving some celtuce for garnish. Arrange the scallop rounds and butternut squash discs in an overlapping pattern around each pile. Pipe dots of the aïoli and purée onto the scallop rounds and butternut squash discs as desired. Arrange the marigolds on top, followed by the remaining celtuce julienne. Pipe more dots of aïoli and purée as desired and serve immediately.

South Korea ⟶ New York, New York

Jae-Eun Jung

At age 29, just as her family expected her to settle down, Jae-Eun Jung left her native Seoul for the US to enroll in the Culinary Institute of America. She would go on to hone her craft at Michelin-starred Oceana and Le Bernardin in New York City and was formally trained in royal court cuisine from the Chosun dynasty in Korea.

After graduation, Jung moved to New Orleans, where she immersed herself in Southern cuisine under African-American icon Chef Leah Chase. Jung says her affinity for New Orleans' deep culinary traditions stemmed from her lifelong love of barbecued pork and seafood, prevalent in Korean menus. She went on to create a dinner theater series entitled, "How Do You Hug a Tiger?" The story of her relationship with her "Tiger Mom" mother in six courses, Jung's menu fused her Korean roots with her love of Southern cooking, featuring Korean and Southern fried chicken with daikon slaw and cornbread and lacquered pork belly with creole tomato kimchi. Jung traveled around the US and held her Korean-New Orleans pop-up events in Chicago, Miami, Austin, Boston, Birmingham, New Orleans, Nashville, and New York. The work was featured in the *New York Times*.

Jung has been working in New York since 2014 at Michelin-starred restaurants including Le Bernardin, where Chef Eric Ripert became her mentor. Her cooking was showcased in a six-course wine pairing dinner series featured on CBS News, *Food & Wine*, *Bon Appétit*, and Eater.

Jung is now a sous chef at the Michelin-starred Café Boulud.

"For me, immigration means to build a home where my hopes and dreams belong."

Jae-Eun Jung

Shrimp and Okra Pancakes and Charred Scallion Dipping Sauce

Serves 4 to 5

After culinary school I cooked in New Orleans, where I fell in love with Southern cuisine and culture. I was trained and mentored by Chef Leah Chase, whom I call my Creole gramma. Cooking with Chef Chase formed the cornerstone of my culinary journey and sparked my creativity. This dish combines Korean and Creole cooking to mutual advantage.

For the tomato kimchi
⅓ cup (75 ml) water
¼ cup (60 ml) fish sauce
¼ cup (60 ml) red wine vinegar
3 cloves garlic, thinly sliced
1 tablespoon granulated sugar
2 firm beefsteak tomatoes, cut into wedges and seeded*
1 large green tomato, cut into wedges and seeded*
*It's important that the tomatoes be firm.

For the dipping sauce
1 teaspoon canola oil
3 scallions
⅓ cup (75 ml) soy sauce
¼ cup (60 ml) rice wine vinegar
1 tablespoon granulated sugar

For the pancakes
1½ cups (200 g) all-purpose flour
1 tablespoon salt
2 cups (480 ml) water
2 large eggs, lightly beaten
1 pound (450 g) medium (41/50 count) shrimp, peeled and deveined
7 okra, cut into ¼-inch-thick (0.5 cm) slices
5 scallions, cut into 1-inch-long (2.5 cm) pieces
Canola oil

For the tomato kimchi
In a medium bowl, combine the water, fish sauce, red wine vinegar, garlic, and sugar and stir vigorously to dissolve the sugar. Add the red and green tomatoes and toss to coat them in the brine then cover and refrigerate for 2 days before you prepare the pancakes. The leftover kimchi can be refrigerated for 1 to 2 weeks.

For the dipping sauce
In a very hot skillet, heat the canola oil and cook the scallions, turning once or twice with tongs, for about 1 minute or until charred. Let the scallions cool then mince and transfer to a small bowl. Add the soy sauce, rice wine vinegar, and sugar and stir to combine.

For the pancakes
In a medium bowl, whisk together the flour and salt. Add the water and eggs and stir to combine. Fold in the shrimp, okra, and scallions.

In a large skillet, heat 2 tablespoons of canola oil over medium heat. Add about ½ cup (120 ml) of the batter and cook for 1 to 2 minutes or until the edges are golden. Flip the pancake and add 1 tablespoon of canola oil to the pan. Move the pancake around to make sure it doesn't scorch on the bottom and cook for about 1 minute or until set. Carefully flip the pancake onto a plate then repeat with more oil and the remaining batter to make additional pancakes. Serve the pancakes with the dipping sauce and tomato kimchi.

Jae-Eun Jung

Soy- and Sugarcane-Glazed Grilled Pork Chops and Tomato-Peach Salad

Serves 4

New Orleans had a huge impact on my life and career, and taught me how important it is to be open, warm, and adventurous. I also found that Korean and Southern cuisines have much in common. Both cultures love barbecue and eat a lot of pork and seafood. Smothering and stewing greens is traditional for both cooking styles and Koreans make kimchi with raw oysters, a Southern staple. I felt so close to home in New Orleans, and was inspired to combine Korean, Cajun, and Creole flavors to create something new.

For the pork chops
4 (7-ounce / 200-g) bone-in pork rib
    chops, each about 1 inch thick
    (2.5 cm)
1½ cups (360 ml) mirin
⅓ cup (75 ml) olive oil
Juice of 2 lemons
7 cloves garlic, crushed
4 sprigs fresh rosemary
1 tablespoon coriander seeds
1 teaspoon black peppercorns
1 teaspoon pink peppercorns

For the grits
1 ear corn, shucked
Canola oil
3 cups (720 ml) water
1 cup (240 ml) heavy cream
1 tablespoon salt
1 cup (140 g) stone-ground grits
¼ cup (60 g) unsalted butter
½ cup (110 g) mascarpone
3 small fresh serrano chiles,
seeded (optional) and diced

For the salad
1 teaspoon canola oil
2 peaches, pitted and cut into
    wedges
¼ cup (60 ml) extra-virgin olive oil
¼ cup (60 ml) gochujang (Korean
    fermented chile bean paste)
2 tablespoons coarse Korean chili
    powder (or other mild chili
    powder, such as
    Piment d'Espelette)
1 tablespoon dark brown sugar
1 tablespoon salt
10 plums, pitted and cut into
    wedges (optional)
1 pint (250 g) cherry tomatoes
1 handful watercress

For the glaze
1 cup (240 ml) soy sauce
½ cup (120 ml) sugarcane syrup,
    such as Steen's
¼ cup (24 g) smoked paprika
3 tablespoons cayenne pepper

For serving
Salt
Fresh mint or cilantro leaves, for
garnish

For the pork chops
Place the pork rib chops in a glass baking dish. In a small bowl, combine the mirin, olive oil, lemon juice, garlic, rosemary, coriander seeds, and black and pink peppercorns. Pour the marinade over the chops, cover, and refrigerate overnight.

For the grits
Light a grill or preheat a grill pan over high heat. Rub the corn with a little canola oil and grill, turning frequently, until charred all over. Let cool then cut the kernels from the cob.

In a heavy, medium saucepan, combine the water, heavy cream, and salt and bring to a boil. Slowly whisk in the grits and continue whisking for 1 minute. Lower the heat and simmer the grits, stirring every few minutes, for 20 to 25 minutes or until tender. Stir in the butter and mascarpone, followed by the grilled corn kernels and serrano chiles. As the grits simmer, make the salad.

Continued $\longrightarrow$

Jae-Eun Jung

For the salad

In a medium skillet, heat the canola oil over medium heat. Add the peaches and cook without turning for about 4 minutes or until golden on 1 side.

In a medium bowl, whisk together the extra-virgin olive oil, gochujang, chili powder, dark brown sugar, and salt. Add the cooked peaches, along with the plums, cherry tomatoes, and watercress, toss, and let stand for 20 minutes.

For the glaze

In a small saucepan, bring the soy sauce, sugarcane syrup, smoked paprika, and cayenne pepper to a boil. Lower the heat and simmer for 5 minutes then let cool until warm.

For serving

Preheat the oven to 400°F (200°C). Light a grill or preheat a grill pan over medium heat.

Remove the pork rib chops from the marinade and scrape off all the spices. Season the chops generously with salt. Grill the chops, turning once, for 5 to 7 minutes or until grill marks appear. Transfer the chops to a roasting pan or baking sheet and brush with the glaze. Roast for about 5 minutes or until the chops look deeply browned and lacquered. Transfer to a cutting board and let rest for 5 minutes.

Spoon the grits onto plates. Set the chops on top of the grits then arrange the salad on top of the chops. Garnish with mint or cilantro and serve.

Ann
Kim

After immigrating from South Korea to Minnesota with her parents and grandmother, Ann Kim grew up eating family dinners that reflected East and West, like KFC and kimchi. Today, she has built on that cross-pollination as a chef and restaurateur with a mini-empire in Minneapolis.

After falling for serious pizza while studying at Columbia University, Kim sought perfection of the form at her first restaurant, Pizzeria Lola. She hadn't intended to put Korean flavors on the menu, but when she topped one pie with kimchi, many Minnesota patrons told her it was their first exposure to the traditional pickle and that the taste had inspired them to explore Korean cuisine in a deeper way.

Her next restaurant was Hello Pizza, followed by Young Joni, whose elevated flavors and diverse, sophisticated menu won her a James Beard Award for Best Chef Midwest in 2019 (she was shortlisted in 2018). Young Joni was also named one of the best new restaurants in the country in 2017 by *GQ,* Eater and others.

Kim calls her cooking "a reflection of my cultural history," and adds that she's not trying to cook inside the lines. "The food that excites me the most is a mix of cultures. Young Joni is really a culmination of my lineage, how I grew up as a Korean-American in Minnesota."

Her next restaurant explores Mexican cuisine. What could be more American than tacos with gochujang?

"I immigrated to the United States with my family as a young child over forty years ago. I'm eternally grateful for my parents who made incredible sacrifices, faced challenges, conquered their fears, and worked tirelessly without complaint in pursuit of endless possibilities for their family. I am proud to work in solidarity with fellow immigrants at our restaurants who contribute to the beautiful fabric of this country and continue to (re)define what it means to be American."

Ann Kim

Grilled Korean-Style Short Ribs with Fresno Pepper Chimichurri and Yogurt

Serves 4

I grew up eating Korean barbecue with my family only on special occasions so this dish sparks many warm and fond memories for me. I wanted to re-create a version of Korean short ribs that also incorporated my love of South American and Middle Eastern flavors. The brightness of the chimichurri and the yogurt is a nice counterpart to the richness of the grilled short ribs.

For the short ribs
7 cloves garlic, peeled
1 Asian pear, peeled, cored, and roughly chopped
½ cup (100 g) granulated sugar
1½ cups (360 ml) low-sodium soy sauce
¼ cup (60 ml) toasted sesame oil
1½ teaspoons freshly ground pepper
3 pounds (1.4 kg) flanken-style short ribs

For the chimichurri
¼ cup (13 g) chopped fresh flat-leaf parsley
2 Fresno chiles, stemmed, seeded, and finely minced
1 teaspoon fresh oregano leaves
½ teaspoon minced garlic
1½ tablespoons red wine vinegar
1 tablespoon extra-virgin olive oil
Salt

For serving
1 cup (240 ml) Greek yogurt

For the short ribs
In a food processor, purée the garlic and Asian pear until smooth. Add the sugar, soy sauce, toasted sesame oil, and pepper and pulse until incorporated. (Alternatively, you can use a blender and purée all of the ingredients at the same time.)

Arrange the short ribs in a large baking dish or 2 large resealable plastic bags. Pour the marinade over the short ribs and turn until fully coated. Cover the baking dish or seal the bags and refrigerate for at least 3 hours or up to 24 hours.

For the chimichurri
In a medium bowl, combine the parsley, Fresno chiles, oregano, garlic, red wine vinegar, and extra-virgin olive oil then season to taste with salt.

For serving
Light a grill or preheat a grill pan over medium-high heat. Working in batches as needed, grill the ribs, turning occasionally, for 4 to 6 minutes for medium-rare to medium, or longer if desired. Spread the Greek yogurt on the bottom of a long serving platter.

Arrange the grilled short ribs on top of the yogurt and drizzle the chimichurri on top. Serve immediately.

"I firmly believe that immigrants are the backbone of this country. I work with many people all here to make their lives better. Now more than ever, it's important to me to represent my culture, my identity, the Filipino people, and I do that with food.

We live in trying times, but I think people will come together and use what tools we have to represent what's best. And the way I know how to do that is through cooking, through food. So I invite everyone to my table."

Philippines ⟶ Portland, Oregon

Carlo Lamagna

Carlo Lamagna's childhood spanned Canada, the Philippines, and Detroit. He felt like an outsider in Detroit, and then felt the same upon returning to the Philippines, where he didn't speak the language and was mocked as an *amboy*.

When Lamagna began his culinary career, he focused not on the Filipino foods he grew up eating, but instead on classical European techniques, an approach that has evolved over time. Today, he believes Filipino cuisine is undergoing a shift in achieving widespread popularity in the United States, and predicts an arc like that of Chinese, Indian, or Thai cuisine. His own menus, which draw on Filipino flavors interpreted through his fine cooking skills, have won him both James Beard attention and a rising star reputation, with Plate naming him a 2018 Chef to Watch.

Lamagna's love of Pacific Northwest seafood means that bay octopus, crab, and salmon are at the center of his menu at his restaurant, MAGNA. For his Twisted Filipino pop-up series, he created dishes using classic techniques and new flavors, starring such ingredients as Dungeness crab, pork skin, nasturtiums, and mushrooms cooked in banana leaves. Beyond the stove, he is committed to cultivating work environments that help chefs and staff thrive.

Carlo Lamagna

My Dad's Pork Adobo

Serves 6 to 8

When I first started cooking, I didn't make Filipino food, but my dad was adamant that I should. He passed away in 2009, and his pork adobo recipe remains very special to me. It's the Filipino national dish, and everyone cooks it a little differently. My dad's version is tart, with extra vinegar (use less if you prefer). He also always waited to add the soy sauce until the very end, so it wouldn't become bitter during the dish's long simmer. It's a simple meal, but to serve it is to share a story. Today I consider it my role as a chef to introduce people to Filipino food and culture the best way I know how, and to make the Filipino people proud, the way my dad wanted me to.

This is a flexible recipe that will work with different cuts of pork, including shoulder, spareribs, pork belly, and neck bones, or a combination of cuts. It's even better the day after it's prepared.

3 tablespoons vegetable oil

3 pounds (1.4 kg) boneless pork shoulder, cubed

8 cloves garlic, peeled

6 bay leaves

1 tablespoon peppercorns

8 cups (1.9 liters) chicken or pork stock

2 cups (480 ml) distilled white vinegar, or less, according to preference

1½ cups (360 ml) soy sauce

Steamed white rice, for serving

In a large, heavy-bottomed saucepan or Dutch oven, heat the vegetable oil over medium-high heat. Working in batches, add the pork shoulder in a single layer and cook, turning, for about 5 minutes or until browned all over. Repeat to brown all the pork shoulder and transfer it to a plate, but leave the saucepan on the heat. Add the garlic, bay leaves, and black peppercorns to the saucepan and cook over medium-high heat for about 1 minute or until fragrant.

Return the pork to the saucepan, add the chicken or pork stock and the distilled white vinegar and bring to a boil, stirring occasionally to scrape up any browned bits from the bottom of the pan. Lower the heat and simmer for 1 to 1½ hours or until the pork is tender and the liquid is reduced by three-quarters. Add the soy sauce and simmer for another 15 minutes or until pork is fork-tender. If you prefer a drier style of adobo, add the soy sauce earlier so it reduces further. Serve with steamed white rice.

Carlo Lamagna

Mom's Noodles: Egg Noodles with Dungeness Crab, Crab Fat, and Peppers

Serves 6

This is a play on the crab noodles my mom always made when I was growing up. The highlight of this dish is the freshwater crab fat, which is the liquid gold of Filipino cuisine. I used to harvest it as a kid, which was a painstaking process, but you can buy crab fat at Asian and Filipino markets. At my restaurant in Oregon, I make a version that stars local Pacific Northwest ingredients, especially our famous Dungeness crab, which I cook for its fat. It's quite delicious.

For the fresh egg noodles
3½ cups (455 g) all-purpose flour
¾ cup plus 1 tablespoon (110 g)
   bread flour
6 ounces (170 g) egg yolk
   (about 9 large egg yolks)
½ cup (120 ml) water
1 teaspoon salt

For the crab fat
1 tablespoon vegetable oil
¼ onion, minced
4 large cloves garlic, minced
1 (1-ounce / 30-g) piece fresh
   ginger, minced
10 ounces (280 g) crab fat
   (taba ng talangka)
2 cups (480 ml) chicken stock
1 fresh serrano chile
Salt and freshly ground pepper

For serving
¾ pound (340 g) picked Dungeness
   crabmeat
Salt and freshly ground pepper
1 Jimmy Nardello pepper (or other
   Italian frying pepper), cut into
   rounds and seeds removed
2 scallions, thinly sliced
Nasturtium leaves and flowers
   (optional)
Microgreens (optional)

For the egg noodles
In the bowl of a stand mixer fitted with the dough hook attachment, sift together the all-purpose and bread flours. Add the egg yolks, water, and salt and knead with the hook on low speed for 10 to 15 minutes or until a dough forms. Loosely cover and let rest for 30 minutes at room temperature.

   Using a pasta maker, roll the dough until ⅛ inch thick (0.25 cm) or even thinner. Cut the dough into 10-inch-long (25 cm) pieces then cut it into ⅛-inch-wide (0.25 cm) noodles. Make the noodles shortly before you mean to cook them.

For the crab fat
In a large, deep saucepan, heat the vegetable oil over medium heat. Add the onion, garlic, and ginger and cook for about 2 minutes or until starting to soften. Add the crab fat and cook for 6 to 8 minutes or until caramelized. Add the chicken stock and serrano chile and bring to a boil. Lower the heat to medium-high and simmer for 15 to 20 minutes or until the liquid is reduced by a quarter. Let cool then discard the chile and season to taste with salt and pepper.

For serving
Bring a large pot of salted water to a boil and cook the noodles for about 2 minutes or until just tender. Drain the noodles and add to the crab sauce. Add the crabmeat and toss to combine. Season to taste with salt and pepper. Transfer the noodles to bowls, top with the thinly sliced pepper and scallions and optionally, nasturtium leaves and flowers plus microgreens, and serve.

"When I first came here I wanted to become Americanized, whatever that means, in so many different ways. Then as I got older, I started to appreciate my native culture more. This return to my origins and the blend that I feel now—that's the American experience.

Food that I'm working with is part of a larger movement for chefs of my generation. Whereas previously, people looked to emulate European cuisine, now we incorporate our personal experience and our culture with the cuisine we are exploring. We're in pursuit of something that's surprisingly delicious, that hasn't been done before."

South Korea ⟶ San Francisco, California

Corey Lee

Seoul-born Corey Lee spent years as head chef at the French Laundry in Napa, when it was widely regarded as the best restaurant in the US. Raised in northern New Jersey, Lee became Chef Thomas Keller's right hand before opening his own modern-haute restaurant, Benu, in San Francisco in 2010. Asian influences are evident in such details as the delicate pleats of crab dumplings, the bright nutty green of autumn gingko crêpes, and the depth of his chrysanthemum broth. But Benu's bold tasting menu transcends categorization. Diners feast on vegetables wrapped to look like glass beads; live jellyfish in beef bouillon with thyme blossoms; and sorbet made of sake lees and finished with strawberry ice and nasturtiums.

No wonder Benu has earned the highest possible culinary honors: four stars from the *San Francisco Chronicle*, the AAA Five Diamond Award, and a stratospheric three Michelin stars. Lee has also become a goodwill ambassador for his hometown of Seoul. His 2015 cookbook showcased Benu's food, inspirations, and the people who make it possible.

Although raised on his parents' Korean home cooking, he recalls disliking kimchi as a child. Now he says, "I think I have a deep-seated desire to take every scorned ingredient I grew up with and make something incredibly delicious out of them."

Corey Lee

Easy Bibimbap for Home

If you "Americanize" any dish from around the world, you might be met with resistance. Some people are purists. But cuisine has always evolved. Bibimbap, which literally means "mixed rice," is one of Korea's most beloved dishes.

For the rice
2¼ cups (450 g) short-grain white rice
1¾ cups (420 ml) water

For the sauce
¼ cup (60 ml) gochujang (Korean fermented chile bean paste)
4 teaspoons water
2 teaspoons dark soy sauce
1¼ teaspoons granulated sugar
1 teaspoon toasted sesame oil

For the vegetables
¼ cup (60 ml) toasted sesame oil
2 medium carrots, cut into rough ¼-inch (0.5 cm) dice
4 large cloves garlic, finely chopped
3 ounces (85 g) shiitake mushrooms, stems removed and caps cut into rough ¼-inch (0.5 cm) dice
1 medium zucchini, cut into rough ¼-inch (0.5 cm) dice
¼ pound (110 g) soy bean sprouts, bottom roots snipped
15 large spinach leaves, stems removed and leaves roughly chopped into large pieces
Salt
2 scallions, thinly sliced into rounds

For the eggs
Vegetable oil
4 large eggs
Salt

For serving
Vegetable oil
Gim (roasted and salted Korean seaweed or use toasted nori), cut into thin strips
10 large sesame leaves (or shiso leaves), cut into strips (optional)
Toasted sesame seeds

For the rice
In a large bowl, soak the rice for 30 minutes in cold water, then rinse until the water runs clear. Drain well.

If you have an electric rice cooker, combine the rice and the 1¾ cups (420 ml) of water and cook according to the manufacturer's instructions. Otherwise, preheat the oven to 375°F (190°C) and bring the rice and water to a boil in a heavy-bottomed saucepan. Cover the pot tightly with a lid and bake for about 20 minutes or until the rice is tender and all the water has been absorbed—the time required for the rice to turn tender and the water to be absorbed will vary depending on the size of the saucepan and the oven's calibration.

For the sauce
In a small bowl, whisk together the gochujang, water, dark soy sauce, sugar, and toasted sesame oil until smooth.

For the vegetables
Heat a large skillet over medium heat. Add the toasted sesame oil, carrots, and garlic and cook for about 2 minutes or until the carrots are almost tender. Add the shiitake mushrooms, zucchini, and soy bean sprouts and cook for 1 to 2 minutes or until just tender. Add the spinach and cook for about 30 seconds or until wilted. All the vegetables should taste cooked but still have a slightly firm texture. Season to taste with salt. Remove from the heat and let cool to room temperature, then stir in the scallions.

For the eggs
Heat a nonstick skillet large enough to hold 4 eggs over medium-high heat. Add a little vegetable oil and cook the eggs until the whites are set and the yolks are still runny. Season lightly with salt.

For serving
Heat a medium cast-iron, enamel, paella, or dolsot pan. When hot, add enough vegetable oil to coat the bottom of the pan. Add the rice and spread it out evenly. Spread the cooked vegetables on top. Add the fried eggs and sprinkle generously with the seaweed, sesame leaves, and sesame seeds. Serve family style with the sauce as a condiment to be added to taste.

Corey Lee

Potato Salad with Anchovy

Most of the food we encounter in the US has been brought here from somewhere else. America's culinary identity has always been forged by immigrants—so there's an openness to what a meal might be. That lack of an anchor actually gives us a little more freedom in the kitchen, more creative opportunity.

When making this dish at the restaurant, we leave the potatoes whole and cook them sous vide. At home, for the best flavor, you can fold the potatoes with the other ingredients while still warm.

For the potato salad
½ cup (120 ml) water
¼ cup (60 ml) red wine vinegar
⅓ cup (65 g) granulated sugar
¼ small red onion, thinly sliced
¾ pound (340 g) Yukon gold
    potatoes, peeled and cut
    into ¼-inch dice (0.5 cm)
2 large eggs
2 celery stalks, very finely
    chopped
⅓ cup plus 1 tablespoon (90 ml)
    mayonnaise
Salt

For the anchovies
¾ cup (150 g) granulated sugar
⅔ cup (150 ml) Champagne vinegar
2 tablespoons plus 2 teaspoons
    tamari
Pinch of cayenne pepper
¾ cup plus 2 tablespoons
    (210 ml) water
2 tablespoons toasted sesame oil
1 clove garlic
3½ ounces (100 g) extra-small
    dried anchovies
⅔ ounce (20 g) finely chopped
    sweet red pepper, rinsed
⅔ ounce (20 g) sesame seeds

For serving
Celery leaves
Julienned fresh red chiles

For the potato salad
In a bowl, vigorously whisk together the water, red wine vinegar, and sugar until the sugar is dissolved. Add the red onion and let stand for 1 hour or cover and refrigerate for up to 3 days.

In a medium saucepan, cover the potatoes with cold water and bring to a boil. Reduce the heat to very low and simmer for 10 to 15 minutes or until just tender. Drain the potatoes then spread them out on a paper towel–lined baking sheet and let cool to warm.

While the potatoes are cooking, fill a medium bowl with ice water and bring a small saucepan of water to a boil. Reduce to a medium simmer and carefully lower the eggs into the water. Cook for exactly 9 minutes, then drain the eggs and transfer to the ice water to cool. Peel and finely chop the eggs.

Fill the saucepan used to cook the potatoes with water and bring to a boil. Place the finely chopped celery in a strainer with a handle then dip the strainer into the boiling water and hold for about 10 seconds or just until the color of the celery changes slightly.

Immediately run the celery under cold water and let dry.

Drain the pickled red onion and finely chop.

In a large bowl, combine the warm potatoes, pickled red onion, eggs, celery, mayonnaise, and ½ teaspoon salt and fold gently to combine. Taste and season with more salt as needed. Refrigerate until chilled.

For the anchovies
In a small saucepan, bring the sugar, Champagne vinegar, tamari, and cayenne to a boil and continue boiling until reduced to a glaze. Add the water and remove from the heat.

In a small skillet, heat the toasted sesame oil and garlic over medium heat. Add the anchovies and cook until lightly caramelized. Add the red pepper, sesame seeds, and enough of the Champagne vinegar glaze to coat. Let cool to room temperature.

For serving
Arrange the anchovies on top of the potato salad, garnish with the celery leaves and julienned chiles, and serve.

"America has an incredible blending of cultures that you just don't have in any other country. That's my whole philosophy of why this is such a special place. That collision will always, always create new combinations, identities, forms of food. If your surroundings are diverse, so will be your art, music, cuisine. You can throw tradition into the wind, and start cooking something very unique. This has been happening since the birth of America.

My family was very upset when I became a chef. My argument was always, 'You brought me to this place where there are freedoms, passions, creative arts. You always said, "Be American." That's what I'm doing.' To me that's what being an immigrant is: trying to hold on to the culture of your mother country, but also start fresh, from scratch, and make the very best of it.

Food is such a beautiful, important gateway, now more than ever. The future of America is going to be driven by the future immigrants who will come. The future is clear for anyone who sees it. The immigrants will drive this country to a better place. Always have. Always will."

South Korea ⟶ Louisville, Kentucky

Edward Lee

Korean-born Edward Lee has found national fame as a chef, success he credits partly to his parents' immigration to Brooklyn. Back in the 1970s, many Asian immigrant families were settling in Queens, but the Lee family decided against a neighborhood with familiar faces, languages and foods, opting instead for the multi-cultural mosaic on the other side of the Brooklyn border.

"'We moved to America, we're gonna become Americans,' my father always said." And so young Lee grew up eating Italian, Jamaican, and many more cuisines all within a few blocks of home, and all of it seemed American. But his parents were also dismayed when he chose to become a chef, telling him, "We didn't come here to scrape and struggle so you can pursue this fantasy."

Today his arc to success seems taken from a textbook on the American dream. Distilling all those melting pot flavors he savored in Brooklyn, he is now chef and owner of three highly acclaimed restaurants in Louisville, Kentucky: 610 Magnolia, MilkWood and Whiskey Dry, and he is culinary director for Succotash in Washington, DC. He hosted the PBS series *Mind of a Chef* and a documentary called *Fermented*, and has been nominated for an Emmy and several James Beard Awards. Lee is also the author of *Smoke & Pickles* and of *Buttermilk Graffiti: A Chef's Journey to Discover America's New Melting-Pot Cuisine*, which won a James Beard Award in 2019.

Edward Lee

Spicy Pork Lettuce Wraps

Serves 4 as an appetizer

I love eating with my hands. It reminds me of the Korean meals I ate as a kid, when we would have a plate of barbecue in front of us accompanied by a mountain of lettuce and a bunch of sides. This is a slightly more refined version of the grazing Korean barbecue menu and is meant to be interactive, so stack the ingredients on the lettuce cups and eat away. The beauty of the dish is that you can add whatever you want—there are limitless variations.

For the pork
½ pound (225 g) pineapple chunks
½ large onion, roughly chopped
1¼ cups (300 ml) gochujang
    (Korean fermented chile
    bean paste)
¾ cup (150 g) light brown sugar
⅓ cup (75 ml) soy sauce
¼ cup (60 ml) toasted sesame oil
8 cloves garlic, minced
3 tablespoons minced fresh ginger
1 tablespoon freshly ground
    pepper
1 (2-pound / 900-g) piece pork belly,
    cut into thin strips

For serving
Canola oil
Gem or butter lettuce leaves,
    separated
Shiso or cilantro leaves
4 asparagus stalks, shaved
    lengthwise with a vegetable
    peeler
Red kimchi
Fried or roasted chickpeas
    (store-bought or homemade)

For the pork
In food processor, purée the pineapple and onion until smooth. Transfer to a large bowl. Add the gochujang, light brown sugar, soy sauce, toasted sesame oil, garlic, ginger, and pepper, and whisk to combine. Add the pork belly and turn to make sure the pieces are well coated in the marinade. Cover and refrigerate for 4 hours.

For serving
Light a grill or preheat a grill pan over high heat. Lightly oil the grates with canola oil.

Arrange the lettuce leaves, shiso leaves, shaved asparagus, red kimchi, and fried chickpeas in individual bowls.

Remove the pork belly from the marinade and grill, turning once, for 1 to 2 minutes per side or until charred but not burnt. Transfer to a plate and invite people to build their own lettuce wraps using the pork, lettuce, and garnishes.

China ⟶ Los Angeles, California and Chicago, Illinois

Johnny Lee

Johnny Lee didn't set out to be a chef, but graduating during the financial crisis put him to work in food. Knowing that hard work would get him noticed, Lee rose through the restaurant ranks, mastering a range of classic and modern French techniques, from sous vide and spherification to foams and vacuum sealing. He applied those skills outside the world of fine dining and soon won Zagat's 30 Under 30 award.

But for Lee, cooking is about more than food. "I realized restaurants' impact on culture, real estate development, and the direction of industry," he recalls. "I began to think that in this industry, we could make meaningful impacts."

It's not just hard work that defines Lee, but also his devotion to quality Cantonese cuisine—and his dedication to a single dish: Hainanese Chicken. Lee has perfected every step of the process. His Buddhist faith informs his commitment to sustainability: he insists on locally sourced, free-range, expertly butchered chickens, and simmers the entire bird in his broth so nothing goes to waste. His results speak for themselves, which is why the late, great Jonathan Gold crowed about Lee's chicken in the *Los Angeles Times*, while *GQ* named Side Chick one of the 10 Best New Restaurants in America.

Having now also opened Chicago's Rakki, Lee says he intends to both preserve and modernize Cantonese cuisine for the next generation.

"It means a lot to me to be an American. In China, there is strong economic and social pressure to pursue a career which pays well in order to lift one's family's societal place— therefore there is often little room for creative thinking or riskier decision making. In America, I feel the freedom to pursue any path. I value my independent freedom more than anything else and strongly believe in American ideals of individualism and entrepreneurialism. I pursued cooking to follow these ideals, but as time went on, I realized that the relevance of Cantonese cooking was diminishing because many of my Cantonese peers chose to follow more conventional career paths. I wanted to keep my culinary heritage alive and strong."

Johnny Lee

Winter Melon Soup

Serves 6 to 8

This is a classic Cantonese soup. There are many variations but the constants are pork bone broth, winter melon, and dried aromatics. If dried squid or scallops are hard to find, try using a similar amount of dried shrimp instead. In fact, feel free to play around with different substitutions for the dried seafood. Winter melon, also known as wax gourd, is seasonal, but you can also make this dish with daikon or opo squash.

If you have a rice cooker that has a warm setting, a neat trick is to allow all the ingredients to slowly simmer overnight, without any risk of overboiling the broth. It's best to use cut spare ribs for the broth, but neck bones will also work.

1 whole dried squid
3 dried scallops
2 tablespoons dried mussels
2 tablespoons dried black-eyed peas
1 piece dried orange or tangerine peel
2 dried Chinese shiitake mushrooms
16 cups (3.8 liters) water, cool
2 pounds (900 g) pork bones
1 ounce (28 g) fresh ginger, sliced
1 pound (450 g) winter melon, peeled and cut into 2-inch (5 cm) cubes
Salt
Shredded dried shrimp, for garnish

In a large bowl, cover the dried seafood, black-eyed peas, orange or tangerine peel, and Chinese shiitake mushrooms with 4 cups (960 ml) of the cool water and let rehydrate overnight.

In a large pot, cover the pork bones with cold water and bring to a boil. Continue boiling for 2 to 3 minutes or until the bones look cooked and gray on the outside. Drain the bones and rinse them in cold water. Clean the pot and fill with the remaining 12 cups (2.8 liters) of cool water. Add the bones again and bring to a simmer. Add the rehydrated ingredients, along with their soaking liquid and the ginger, and bring to a simmer. Continue simmering for at least 2 hours or ideally as long as 6 hours. Between 1 and 2 hours before you wish to drink the soup, add the winter melon and allow it to slowly cook until it is as soft as tofu. Transfer the winter melon to serving bowls and strain the broth, discarding the solids. Season the broth to taste with salt, ladle into bowls, garnish with shredded dried shrimp, and serve.

Johnny Lee

Crispy Soy Chicken

Serves 3 to 4

If you have access to young brown chicken, which may be labeled "Indian" chicken, use one of those. They tend to be less tender than the common white pullet breeds, but they're more flavorful and their thick skin will crisp up nicely. If you can't find head-on chicken, a poultry hook will make the recipe easier.

1 whole chicken, about 3 pounds (1.4 kg), preferably head on and free-range (or 3 pounds / 1.4 kg whole chicken wings)
Salt
16 cups (3.8 liters) chicken stock (or water)
8 cups (1.9 liters) soy sauce
14 ounces (400 g) maltose (or honey or corn syrup)
2 ounces (60 g) fresh ginger, sliced
1 bunch scallions
Canola oil, for frying

Rub the chicken all over with salt and let stand at room temperature for 1 hour or refrigerate overnight.

In a large saucepan, bring the chicken stock, soy sauce, maltose, ginger, and scallions to a boil. Hold the chicken by the neck or by a poultry hook and carefully dip it into the hot liquid to fill the inside cavity—this will help the chicken cook more evenly. Add the chicken to the pot again then turn off the heat and let steep for 20 minutes. Using an instant-read thermometer, monitor the temperature of the breast. If it starts to creep past 135°F (57°C), pull the chicken from the pot. Transfer the chicken to a work surface and let cool slightly.

Preheat the oven to 300°F / 150°C (preferably convection setting).

Set a rack inside a roasting pan and place the chicken on top. Bake for 20 minutes to 1 hour or until an instant-read thermometer inserted in the inner thigh reaches 165°F (75°C)—the time will vary depending on the size of the chicken, how much it cooked in the broth, and whether or not convection is used. Let cool to room temperature then refrigerate, without covering, overnight—this will dry out the skin and help make it more crisp.

The next day, preheat the oven to 300°F (150°C) and warm the chicken in the oven for about 10 minutes then remove and pat it dry all over, including inside the cavity.

In a wok or a heavy-bottomed pan, heat 2 to 4 inches (5 to 10 cm) of canola oil to 375 to 400°F (190 to 200°C). Carefully add the chicken to the hot oil and fry, turning occasionally, until the skin is crisp. Transfer the chicken to a rack and let rest for about 5 minutes then season to taste with salt, carve, and serve.

China ⟶ Washington, DC

Binhong Lu

Binhong Lu helped usher in a culinary renaissance to the US capital, transforming the DC dining scene from pork-barrel lobbyists doing steakhouse deals to a new world: two-Michelin-star cuisine at the groundbreaking restaurant Pineapple and Pearls, where he is head chef.

What's even more American than that? Perhaps the story of Lu himself, who was born in China but grew up criss-crossing the US as his father trained as an engineer. A child frequently on the move, Lu learned to integrate with the community, often relying on meals for "precious common ground." Eventually, he set out for a serious culinary career and rose like a rocket.

In its stunning four-star review, the *Washington Post* described Pineapple and Pearls as "lofty dinner theater, 'Hamilton' for the taste buds." The seasonal menu offers prix-fixes courses featuring such ingredients as marigold petals and crispy turbot skin, plus Lu's outrageously playful dessert creation comprising black truffle–infused soft-serve ice cream with rainbow gummy bears, shiro dashi whipped cream, and sturgeon caviar.

Lu is passionately committed to the restaurant's model of empowering workers by investing in their language skills and financial futures. The hospitality and luxury of the James Beard Award–finalist's kitchen translate into paid staff vacation time and something almost unheard of in the restaurant world: weekends off.

"At the end of the day we were all immigrants, and I believe we are all working for the same thing: happiness and fulfillment for ourselves and those we love."

Binhong Lu

Wagyu Beef Tartare with Oyster Cream, Corn Pudding, and Tomatoes

At the restaurant, we're able to purchase an extremely high grade of beef with the maximum amount of internal fat. It's tender enough that we barely need to trim it at all. If you're not able to get wagyu tenderloin, opt for a fully trimmed piece of beef tenderloin and dice it finely. When we serve this dish, we make a tea using the leftover parts of the corn, garnished with lovage oil and black winter truffles. We also cure, smoke, and dry beef hearts to grate over this dish to lend a final touch of seasoning and texture. Bonito flakes, readily available in the Asian section of most grocery stores, will do the trick at home.

For the semi-dried tomatoes
1 pint (250 g) cherry tomatoes

For the corn pudding
4 large ears corn
Salt
Freshly squeezed lime juice

For the oyster cream
15 briny oysters, such as Wild Ass Pony oysters from Maryland's Assateague Island
½ tablespoon unsalted butter
1 medium shallot, thinly sliced
¼ cup (60 ml) brandy
¼ cup (60 ml) heavy cream
Freshly ground pepper
Freshly squeezed lemon juice
Salt

For the beef tartare
1 tablespoon diced beef fat
1½ pounds (680 g) beef tenderloin, preferably wagyu or other well-marbled beef, finely diced
Freshly squeezed lemon juice
Salt
Katsuobushi (bonito flakes), for garnish

For the semi-dried tomatoes
Preheat the oven to 250°F (120°C).
Spread the tomatoes in single layer on a baking sheet and bake, checking every hour or so, for 3 to 4 hours or until the tomatoes are partially dried out—they should look leathery and not yield any juice when squeezed. Let cool then roughly chop.

For the corn pudding
Shuck the corn then use a serrated knife to cut the kernels from the cobs. (Discard the cobs and husks or reserve to make a corn cob tea.)
In a food processor, purée the corn kernels until smooth. Transfer the corn purée to a medium pot and set over low heat. Cook, whisking occasionally and lowering the heat as needed to prevent the corn from scorching on the bottom, for about 2 hours or until the purée is reduced by half and has a pudding-like consistency. Season to taste with salt and lime juice.

For the oyster cream
Shuck the oysters, reserving and straining the liquor. In a small saucepan, melt the butter over medium heat. Add the shallot and cook, stirring, for about 2 minutes or until soft and translucent. Add the reserved oyster liquor and brandy, bring to a boil, and reduce by half. Add the heavy cream and bring to a simmer. Add the oysters and remove from the heat.
Transfer the oyster mixture to a blender and season to taste with pepper. Blend the oyster cream then season to taste with lemon juice and salt. Keep warm.

For the beef tartare
In a medium skillet, melt the beef fat over medium heat. Add the diced beef tenderloin, toss, season to taste with lemon juice and salt, and remove from the heat. Add the chopped semi-dried tomatoes and toss to combine.
In each of 8 shallow bowls, make a small pool of oyster cream, using about ¼ cup (60 ml) of cream per bowl. Mound the beef on top then add a generous amount of corn pudding. Cover the entire surface with katsuobushi and serve, advising guests to combine everything before eating.

Argentina ⟶ Washington, DC

Daniela Moreira

Daniela Moreira graduated from the Culinary Institute of America (CIA) in New York but her culinary education began as a child in Argentina, cooking over fire. Her parents ran a campground and, starting at a young age, she helped her mother and grandmother make pastries, bread, pizza, empanadas and more—all cooked outdoors over an open flame.

In pursuit of a culinary career, Moreira staged at restaurants in Italy before moving to Washington, DC, where she worked full-time as an au pair while also attending a culinary arts academy. She won a scholarship to the CIA and, upon completion of the two-year program, cooked at Eleven Madison Park, hailed as the best restaurant in the world.

When Moreira was back in DC, having accepted a position at a new fine dining retaurant there, a chance encounter at the farmers market drew her back to cooking over fire. She struck up a conversation with owners of a wood-oven pizza business and left with an offer. ("I had to go home and google what a 'gig' is," she laughs.) Soon she was googling "equity," too, as the owners made her chef-partner.

Timber Pizza's owners aren't the only ones impressed with Moreira's ways with flame and flavor. That year (2017), *Bon Appétit* named Timber one of the Best New Restaurants in America. Her fire-kissed pies were also named Best Pizza in America.

"DC is a whole beautiful community, people from all over the world, so many immigrants. Here you can learn from each other and help each other. I always knew that Argentinian food has influences from Italy, Germany, and more, and it's the same here. More so. This is what makes American food so great. I was so lucky to get all these opportunities, and now I get to be the one that shows everybody else that it's possible."

Daniela Moreira

Corn Empanadas with Spicy Jam

Makes 10 empanadas

When I was little, my mom made the best corn empanadas. She and my grandmothers taught me how to make this Argentinian classic and they've been on the menu at Timber since day one. The recipe calls for a smoked paprika used everywhere in Argentina. These can be served at room temperature, but they're even better warm. I cook these over a wood fire, but here's a home oven version.

For the spicy jam
4 cups (580 g) seasonal fruit, any pits removed
2 cups (400 g) granulated sugar
1 cup (150 g) roughly chopped fresh chiles
1 tablespoon freshly squeezed lime juice

For the dough
½ cup plus 1 tablespoon (135 ml) water
1 teaspoon salt
2 tablespoons lard
2 cups (260 g) all-purpose flour
1 large egg

For the filling
½ tablespoon olive oil
1 tablespoon finely chopped red onion
1 tablespoon finely chopped bell pepper
2 cups (290 g) fresh corn kernels
Salt
½ teaspoon red pepper flakes
½ teaspoon smoked paprika
1 tablespoon finely chopped scallion

For the spicy jam
In a large saucepan, bring the fruit, sugar, chiles, and lime juice to a boil, stirring. Lower the heat and simmer, stirring occasionally, until the mixture looks jammy but not too thick. Fill a large bowl with ice water and carefully set the saucepan into the ice water to cool the jam. Transfer the cooled jam to a sealable container or jar and refrigerate for up to 1 month.

For the dough
In a small saucepan, bring ½ cup (240 ml) of the water and the salt to a simmer. Add the lard and stir until melted. Transfer to the bowl of a stand mixer fitted with the dough hook attachment, add the flour, and mix for about 5 minutes or until a smooth dough forms. (Alternatively, mix and knead the dough by hand.) Cover the bowl with plastic wrap and refrigerate for about 1 hour. While the dough is chilling, make the filling.

For the filling
In a medium saucepan, heat the olive oil over medium-high heat. Add the red onion and bell pepper and cook, stirring, for about 3 minutes or until softened. Add the corn and cook, stirring, for 3 to 5 minutes or until tender. Season to taste with salt then stir in the red pepper flakes and smoked paprika. In a food processor or blender, or with an immersion blender, purée until the corn kernels are broken down then stir in the scallion.

For serving
Preheat the oven to 450°F (230°C).

On a floured work surface, use a rolling pin to roll out the dough until ⅛-inch thick (0.25 cm). Let rest for a few minutes then use a 4-inch (10 cm) biscuit cutter or drinking glass to cut the dough into about 10 rounds.

Spoon about 1 tablespoon of the filling in the center of each round and fold the rounds up and over the filling to form a half moon. Pinch the edges together to seal. (There might be a little filling left over.)

In a small bowl, whisk the egg with the remaining 1 tablespoon of water.

Spread the empanadas on a baking sheet, brush with the egg wash, and bake for about 15 minutes or until golden brown. Serve warm or at room temperature with the spicy jam.

Daniela Moreira

The Lulu

I grew up cooking outside with my mother, making everything over the fire, including pizza. That's the way we do it at Timber, too. This recipe features several cheeses, including mozzarella, ricotta salata, provolone, and a cheese from Argentina called *Reggianito*, but you can substitute Parmesan.

For the dough
2 cups plus 2 tablespoons (270 g) high-gluten flour
1¼ teaspoons salt
1½ teaspoons granulated sugar
½ teaspoon instant yeast
1½ tablespoons olive oil
⅔ cup (150 ml) water, cold

For the pizzas
1 pint (250 g) Sun Gold tomatoes
2 cloves garlic, minced
3 tablespoons olive oil
4 teaspoons dried oregano
¼ pound (110 g) whole milk mozzarella, shredded
¼ pound (110 g) aged provolone, shredded
2 ounces (60 g) ricotta salata, shredded
2 ounces (60 g) Reggianito (or Parmesan), shredded
Fresh purple basil leaves, for garnish

For the dough
In the bowl of a food processor or a stand mixer fitted with the paddle attachment, mix together the high-gluten flour, salt, sugar, and yeast. With the machine on, add the olive oil and cold water. If using a stand mixer, switch to the dough hook attachment. Mix for about 1 minute in the food processor and 5 minutes in the stand mixer or until the dough forms a smooth ball and is no longer sticky. (Alternatively, mix and knead the dough by hand.)

Using a dough cutter, cut the dough in half. Gently knead each piece into a smooth ball without any creases or holes. Put the balls in 2 separate bowls, cover, and refrigerate for 2 to 3 days.

For the pizzas
Remove the dough from the refrigerator 2 hours before you plan to bake the pizzas. Set a pizza stone or a rimless baking sheet on the bottom rack of the oven and remove the top rack of the oven. Preheat the oven to 450°F (230°C) for at least 1 hour with the pizza stone and 15 minutes with the baking sheet.

On a baking sheet, toss the sun gold tomatoes and garlic with 2 tablespoons of the olive oil and 2 teaspoons of the oregano. Place the baking sheet on the preheating pizza stone or baking sheet and roast for 15 to 20 minutes or until the tomatoes burst and start to collapse. Remove the tomatoes from the oven and raise the temperature to 500°F (260°C).

Generously dust a work surface with flour then gently stretch each ball of dough into a roughly 12-inch (30 cm) round. Generously dust a pizza peel or rimless baking sheet with flour and transfer 1 round of dough to the peel. Working quickly, drizzle the round of dough with ½ tablespoon of the olive oil then sprinkle with ½ of the mozzarella, provolone, ricotta salata, and Reggianito and 1 teaspoon of the oregano. As you work, shake the peel occasionally to prevent the dough from sticking. Slide the pizza onto the hot pizza stone or baking sheet in the oven and carefully top with half of the tomatoes. Bake for 10 to 15 minutes or until the dough is golden brown and the cheese is melted. Using tongs, transfer the pizza back to the peel and remove from the oven. Slide onto a serving board or work surface and top with the purple basil before slicing and serving. Repeat to make the second pizza.

Laos ⟶ Raleigh, North Carolina

Vansana Nolintha

"I cannot comprehend the breadth of my parents' hearts and the depth of their soul that gave them the courage and strength to send me and my sister to the United States so that we could live better lives.

Now my goal is to create positive impacts in my communities through food. I believe that food can facilitate and lead to meaningful social, political, and economic change. At our restaurants, we work hard to create a culture centered in generosity, positivity, and empathy. For the past six years, we have been working with the US Committee for Refugees and Immigrants—training and employing newcomers and providing them the experiences and relationships needed to become dignified leaders in their communities. I believe that in order for us to build a world rooted in empathy and kindness, we must build bridges in our communities. Food and hospitality are my mediums in the construction of that bridge. Food is revealing as it exposes our love, loss, memory, hope, and fear."

Vansana Nolintha was born in Laos, but his parents' prayers were realized when they obtained an American visa for him and sent their twelve-year-old son to live in the US. When Nolintha's sister, Vanvisa, followed a few years later, he raised her himself. The two siblings built a life in North Carolina but maintained a connection to family back home through foods their grandmother and mother had cooked, like sticky rice and fish stews.

Nolintha's education spanned chemistry, art, global service-learning, and volunteering on gender-based violence prevention. While studying International Peace and Conflict Studies in Dublin, his life pivoted on a crucial realization: he began to see the power of food in creating community and its role in human spirituality. He decided to open a restaurant.

To finance Bida Manda, the first Laotian restaurant in Raleigh, North Carolina—indeed one of few in all of the US—Nolintha's parents sold a plot of family land in Laos. Soon Raleigh residents were enjoying flavors from the Mekong, including green papaya salad and crispy pork belly stew, surrounded by family portraits and a wooden installation Nolintha created in art school. Maintaining peace as a core value, Bida Manda supports refugee programs and efforts to address addiction and homelessness. But many people come simply for the food, which earned the restaurant a place as a James Beard Award semifinalist. The restaurant developed such a strong following that it led to a spinoff: Brewery Bhavana. *Bon Appétit* called it a showstopper and named it one of its 2017 Hot Ten, the list of Best New Restaurants in the country.

Vansana Nolintha

Crispy Rice Lettuce Wraps

Serves 6 to 8

My sister and I opened Bida Manda, whose name is Sanskrit for "father and mother," as a gathering place celebrating our Laotian cooking tradition, as well as our memories of and reverence for home. The menu is an extension of stories rooted in our parents' cooking, and inspired by the many teachers, mentors, travels, and institutions I am fortunate to have in my life. In a way, Bida Manda is an American story, one that engages with fundamental questions surrounding truth, identity, hope, and what it means to try to understand one another during a time of such great divide. It is both a love letter to our parents and a lifelong gesture of gratitude to this country that has given us so much.

In this dish, cooked rice is combined with eggs, coconut, and curry paste, then pressed into patties and fried until golden. Serve the crispy rice in lettuce leaves with cilantro, mint, chili sauce, and peanuts.

For the sweet chili sauce
1 cup (200 g) granulated sugar
2 cups (480 ml) water
¼ cup (60 ml) fish sauce
Juice of 1 lime
2 fresh Thai chiles, crushed
1 teaspoon salt

For the lettuce wraps
1¼ cups (250 g) jasmine rice, cooked
½ cup (40 g) finely shredded dried
   unsweetened coconut
2 large eggs, lightly beaten
2 tablespoons red curry paste
1 tablespoon salt
6 cups (1.4 liters) vegetable oil
¼ cup (50 g) granulated sugar
¼ cup (60 ml) fish sauce
   (or 2 teaspoons salt for
   a vegetarian version)
Juice of 2 limes
1 cup (40 g) chopped fresh cilantro
   leaves
½ cup (25 g) chopped fresh mint
   leaves
½ cup (75 g) chopped roasted and
   salted peanuts
4 heads romaine or Bibb lettuce,
   leaves separated

For the sweet chili sauce
Heat a medium saucepan over medium-low heat. Add the sugar and stir for 3 to 5 minutes or until the sugar starts to melt and slightly caramelize. Be extremely attentive, as the sugar can easily burn. Add the water, raise the heat to medium-high, and cook, stirring occasionally, for 5 to 10 minutes or until the sugar is completely dissolved. Pour the syrup into a bowl and refrigerate for 15 minutes. Add the fish sauce, lime juice, Thai chiles, and salt and stir until combined. Set aside some sauce for serving. The leftover sauce can be refrigerated in a resealable container or jar for several weeks.

For the lettuce wraps
In a large bowl, combine the jasmine rice, shredded coconut, eggs, red curry paste, and salt and mix together thoroughly. Tightly press the rice mixture into 4 patties.

In a large, deep skillet or wide, heavy-bottomed saucepan, heat the vegetable oil over medium-high heat until just starting to shimmer. Add the rice patties and cook, turning once, for 3 to 5 minutes per side or until golden brown all over. Transfer to a paper towel—lined plate and let rest for 15 minutes.

In a large, clean bowl, whisk together the sugar, fish sauce, and lime juice until the sugar is dissolved. Break up the rice cakes into small pieces and add to the bowl. Add the cilantro, mint, and peanuts and toss until evenly dressed. Serve the crispy rice mixture with the lettuce leaves for wrapping and sweet chili sauce.

Vansana Nolintha

Cilantro Rice Chicken Congee

Serves 4 to 6

By cooking and sharing, we choose to be brave, exposing our truth with the hope that it becomes an invitation for others to share theirs, too. I believe that is how we arrive at empathy together.

3 ounces (85 g) fresh ginger
15 cups (3.6 liters) water
1 to 1½ pounds (450 to 680 g) whole chicken legs
1 small handful fresh cilantro stems, tied with kitchen string, plus chopped cilantro for serving
2 tablespoons salt
1 tablespoon chicken bouillon (or mushroom powder)
Granulated sugar
1½ cups (285 g) jasmine rice, washed and drained
½ cup (120 ml) vegetable oil
½ head garlic, cloves finely chopped
2 tablespoons Thai chili flakes
Chopped scallions, quartered limes, freshly ground pepper, and soy sauce, for serving

Heat a cast-iron pan over high heat or set the oven to broil. Put the ginger in the pan or under the broiler and cook, turning occasionally, for about 10 minutes or until well charred.

In a large stock pot, bring the water to a boil. Add the charred ginger, the chicken legs, cilantro stems, salt, chicken bouillon, and a pinch of sugar and cook for 20 minutes. Lower the heat to medium, add the jasmine rice, and cook, stirring occasionally, for 30 to 40 minutes or until the rice has a porridge-like consistency.

As the congee cooks, heat the vegetable oil in a small skillet over medium heat. Add the garlic and cook, stirring, for 1 to 2 minutes or until golden. Add the chili flakes and cook for 10 seconds or until fragrant. Pour into a small bowl for serving.

Remove and discard the cilantro stems and ginger from the congee. Remove the chicken legs and let cool slightly. Once the chicken is cool enough to handle, pull off the meat and return it to the pot.

Serve the congee with the garlic-chile oil, the chopped cilantro, and additional sugar, plus the scallions, limes, pepper, and soy sauce, so people can adjust their bowls to taste.

Philippines ⟶ Los Angeles, California

Charles Olalia

Philippines-born Charles Olalia was focused squarely on fine dining when a return to his home country for his wedding inspired him to rethink his cooking.

His background in elevated cuisine at restaurants like Guy Savoy in Las Vegas and Patina in Los Angeles—and his work with superstar chefs Thomas Keller, Daniel Patterson, and Robbie Lewis—had taken his skills to the highest level. After his wedding, he decided to marry the flavors of his childhood with those fine-dining techniques, and began incorporating references to traditional Filipino dishes into his cooking. He came back to California and opened the tiny Rice Bar with a partner in downtown Los Angeles, earning widespread acclaim. He followed it with Ma'am Sir, named for the traditional greeting heard in the markets of Manila. Seven-seat Rice Bar gets raves for its menu built around heirloom rice, while Ma'am Sir has generated excitement for its Filipino comfort food paired with craft cocktails. One of Olalia's goals in life was to mentor a younger chef. Now that younger chef runs Rice Bar.

Olalia had earned a degree in biology but found kitchens more rewarding, he says. While the culinary arts are not highly regarded in his native country, coming to the United States allowed him to excel.

"Being an immigrant has given me the golden opportunity to work in the United States. When I was in the Philippines, the culinary arts were not a respected profession. Moving stateside has allowed me to learn, practice, and gain valuable experience I could not have gained if I stayed in the Philippines. The kitchen is a melting pot of cultures. I have learned so much from chefs and cooks from different countries, all immigrants, all with the same goal of bettering their careers and their lives."

Charles Olalia

Sea Urchin Lumpia

Makes about 4 dozen

Lumpia is the most commonly eaten snack in the Philippines. When I started cooking Filipino food, I actually didn't put this on our menu, because everyone already knows about it. What I didn't realize was that there is so much creativity to infuse into these fried morsels. Lumpia is usually made with shrimp and pork. We use a shrimp mousse speckled with pork back fat, scallions, and black pepper.

2 pounds (900 g) large (31/35 count) shrimp, peeled and deveined
1 (roughly 4½-ounce / 130 g) tray shelled fresh uni (sea urchin)
2 tablespoons extra-virgin olive oil
2 tablespoons dark soy sauce
2 tablespoons toasted sesame oil
2 tablespoons sherry vinegar
1 tablespoon calamansi or rice vinegar
¼ cup plus 3 tablespoons (90 g) granulated sugar
2½ teaspoons salt
2 teaspoons freshly ground pepper
10 large egg whites
8 scallions, thinly sliced
7 ounces (200 g) pork back fat, diced
1 (¾-pound / 340 g) package spring roll wrappers
Canola oil
Lime wedges and thinly sliced chives, for serving

In a food processor, pulse the shrimp, ½ of the uni, the extra-virgin olive oil, dark soy sauce, toasted sesame oil, sherry vinegar, calamansi vinegar, sugar, salt, pepper, and 2 of the egg whites for about 6 minutes or until it has the light texture of a mousseline. (Depending on the size of your food processor, you may need to do this in 2 batches.) Transfer to a large bowl then add the scallions and pork back fat and gently fold them into the mousseline. Transfer to a piping bag fitted with a medium to large plain tip.

Line a baking sheet with parchment paper.

In a large bowl, whisk the remaining 8 egg whites until foamy. On a clean work surface, arrange 1 spring roll wrapper so one of the points is facing you. Brush the entire surface with the foamy egg whites. Pipe about 1 tablespoon of the filling on the bottom half and fold the bottom corner over the filling. Fold up the sides then tightly roll up the spring roll wrapper into a tight cigar to completely enclose the filling. Transfer to the parchment-lined baking sheet and cover with plastic wrap while you roll the remaining lumpia. You may have a few wrappers left over.

In a large, heavy saucepan or Dutch oven, heat 3 inches (7.5 cm) of canola oil to 350°F (180°C). Set a rack inside a baking sheet, line the rack with paper towels, and arrange it near the stove. Working in batches, carefully add just enough lumpia so they can bob around freely in the hot oil, and fry, turning occasionally, for about 2½ minutes or until golden brown. Using tongs, transfer the lumpia to the rack to drain. Repeat to fry the remaining lumpia.

Serve the lumpia with the remaining uni, the lime wedges, and chives.

Charles Olalia

Banana Bibingka

Bibingka is a rice cake popular in the Philppines, and eaten throughout the day. It can be made with whole rice kernels or rice flours. We like to combine the flavors of coconut and bananas, something we always ate growing up. Garnish with a dusting of confectioners' sugar, some rose petals, and whipped cream.

For the batter
4 large eggs
3 cups (600 g) granulated sugar
1 (14-ounce / 414 ml) can coconut milk
1½ cups (360 ml) evaporated milk
4 cups (850 g) mochiko (sweet rice flour)
1 tablespoon plus 1 teaspoon baking powder
1¼ teaspoons salt

For the bananas
¼ cup (50 g) granulated sugar
¼ cup (60 ml) water
4 ripe bananas, peeled and sliced

For the batter
In a large bowl, beat the eggs and sugar with an electric mixer on medium-high speed until light and fluffy. Add the coconut milk, evaporated milk, and mochiko, alternating between the liquid and flour in 3 batches and ending with the mochiko. Add the baking powder and salt and beat until incorporated.

For the bananas
In a large, heavy saucepan, bring the sugar and water to a boil. Add the bananas then reduce the heat to low and cook until the bananas are soft. Let cool completely then fold the cooled bananas into the batter.

Preheat the oven to 375°F (190°C). Line a 9 x 13-inch (23 x 33 cm) baking pan with parchment paper leaving a 1-inch (2.5 cm) overhang on both long sides. Using an offset spatula, spread the batter evenly in the pan then bake for about 30 minutes or until a cake tester comes out clean. Let cool for about 15 minutes, then use the parchment paper to lift the cake out of the pan and onto a rack and let cool. Cut into squares and serve.

Thailand ⟶ Washington, DC

Pichet Ong

Pichet Ong is of Chinese descent, grew up in Thailand and Singapore, and moved with his family to New York at age fourteen. He earned a master's degree in architecture from the University of California at Berkeley, but instead built a career as a self-taught chef.

Ong combines the flavors of his travels with classic techniques to create sweet and savory foods that are simultaneously whimsical, experimental, and nostalgic. He's been featured in *Food & Wine, Saveur,* the *New York Times, W, Elle, Vogue*, and *O, The Oprah Magazine*, and named one of the Top Ten Pastry Chefs in America in *Pastry Arts & Design*. His desserts have received multiple three-star reviews in the *New York Times*, a Michelin star, and placement in the World's 50 Best Restaurants list. He has been nominated multiple times for awards by the James Beard Foundation, has been a regular judge on Bravo's *Top Chef* and his book, *The Sweet Spot*, was praised in the *New York Times*, *Gourmet*, and *World Gourmand*.

Ong now lives in Northern Virginia but his food can be found worldwide, in as far-flung spots as New York, Sydney, Istanbul, Beijing, Tokyo, and Washington, DC.

"As a curious cook, I've always been fascinated by the different ways people approach food, and the myriad roles it plays in our lives. In the kitchen, I embrace a world not defined by borders, but rather by ideas that stem from a constant migration of all culinary foodways. Just as my family is not related by genes, but bound by a mutual love and celebration of diverse cultures. We are all one family in my world."

Pichet Ong

The Mykonos

From high-volume steakhouses to eponymous Asian restaurants, with a few intimate dessert bars in between, "cheesecake" has prevailed on menus. At Brothers and Sisters in the LINE Hotel DC, I couldn't make up my mind which version I wanted—from firm New York–style to soft and super aerated, from no-bake to the steamed variety, which is loved far and beyond in Asia. Ultimately, I decided to combine them all into one entity called the Mykonos, a Greek island famous for its visually stunning windmills and pristine white stucco.

I recommend making this dessert from beginning to end in one uninterrupted shot. It's important to use the right cheeses, such as super soft and mild Laura Chenel chèvre from Sonoma, and milky rich Cabot crème fraîche from Vermont. When in doubt, I always say to taste the cheeses before using.

For the crust
9 ounces (250 g) gluten-free graham crackers or other plain cookies, broken into pieces
2 tablespoons (30 g) unsalted butter, melted and cooled
½ teaspoon (2 g) Maldon salt
Nonstick cooking spray

For the rice flour cake
3½ ounces (100 g) egg yolks
¼ cup plus 3 tablespoons plus 1 teaspoon (95 g) granulated sugar
½ teaspoon (2 g) fine salt
3 tablespoons (45 ml) buttermilk
3 tablespoons (45 ml) grapeseed oil
½ teaspoon (2 g) vanilla paste
¼ cup plus 2 teaspoons (35 g) cornstarch
¼ cup (35 g) rice flour
5 ounces (140 g) egg whites

For the cream cheese soufflé
⅔ cup (155 g) cream cheese
2 tablespoons (30 g) unsalted butter
¼ cup (60 ml) buttermilk
¼ cup plus 2 tablespoons plus 2 teaspoons (85 g) granulated sugar
¾ teaspoon (3 g) vanilla paste
Zest and juice of ½ lemon
½ teaspoon (2 g) fine salt
2½ ounces (70 g) egg yolks
3 tablespoons (22 g) cornstarch
2½ tablespoons (22 g) rice flour
4¼ ounces (120 g) egg whites

For the chèvre cheesecake mousse
1½ cups (360 ml) heavy cream
½ ounce (15 g) silver-grade gelatin sheets
¾ cup plus 1 tablespoon (195 ml) crème fraîche
2 tablespoons (30 ml) honey
1¾ cups plus 3 tablespoons (450 g) cream cheese
1½ cups (380 g) chèvre
¾ cup plus 1 tablespoon plus 1 teaspoon (170 g) granulated sugar
Zest and juice of ½ lemon
1 teaspoon (4 g) fine salt

For the crust
Preheat the oven to 350°F (180°C). Cut parchment paper to fit the bottom of a 9.5-inch (24 cm) springform pan so the parchment overhangs about 1½ inches (4 cm) all the way around. Cut a 3-inch-wide (7.5 cm) strip to line the sides of the pan. Spray both sides of the parchment round and strip with nonstick cooking spray and arrange them in the pan.

In a food processor, pulse the graham crackers until finely chopped, then process until fine crumbs form. Transfer to a medium bowl. Add the melted and cooled butter and the Maldon salt and mix and crumble with your hands until the mixture resembles wet sand.

Press the crumb mixture firmly on the bottom of the prepared pan and bake for about 7 minutes or until golden. Let cool completely. Wrap the bottom and sides of the pan with aluminum foil, making sure the foil comes all the way up the sides of the pan.

Continued ⟶

For the rice flour cake

Preheat the oven to 350°F (180°C). Line the bottom of an 8-inch (20 cm) round cake pan with a 9-inch (23 cm) round of parchment paper. Do not spray.

In a large bowl, whisk together the egg yolks, 2 tablespoons (25 g) of the sugar, the fine salt, buttermilk, grapeseed oil, and vanilla paste. Sift the cornstarch and rice flour over the egg yolk mixture and stir to incorporate until no streaks remain. Let stand while you prepare the egg whites.

In a stand mixer fitted with the whisk attachment, beat the egg whites for about 3 minutes or until foamy. Gradually add the remaining ¼ cup plus 4 teaspoons (70 g) sugar and beat for about 7 minutes or until medium-stiff peaks form.

Add half of the beaten egg whites to the egg yolk mixture and stir to lighten the texture then add the remaining egg whites, gently folding until no streaks remain. Transfer the batter to the prepared pan and bake for about 24 minutes or until the top of the cake is golden brown with a slight crack and a cake tester inserted in the center comes out clean. (Check the cake halfway through baking and if it's browning too fast, reduce the temperature to 325°F / 160°C.) Let the cake cool for 10 minutes then invert onto a work surface and remove the parchment. Let cool completely.

For the cream cheese soufflé

Set a rack in the center of the oven and preheat the oven to 330°F / 165°C (or 325°F / 160°C if necessary; not convection).

Bring a kettle of water to a boil and keep hot.

Set a medium bowl over a medium pot of simmering water. Add the cream cheese, butter, buttermilk, 3 tablespoons (40 g) of the sugar, the vanilla paste, lemon juice and zest, and fine salt and whisk until homogenous.

Remove the bowl from the heat and whisk in the egg yolks. Sift the cornstarch and rice flour over the cream cheese mixture then whisk to combine. Let stand about 10 minutes or until the flour and cornstarch dissolve.

Meanwhile, in a stand mixer fitted with the whisk attachment, beat the egg whites for about 3 minutes or until foamy. Gradually add the remaining 3 tablespoons plus 1 teaspoon (45 g) sugar and beat for about 7 minutes or until medium-stiff peaks form.

Add one third of the beaten egg whites to the cream cheese mixture and stir to lighten the texture then add the remaining egg whites, gently folding until no streaks remain.

Pour the batter over the crust in the springform pan. Set the pan in a 1-inch-deep (2.5 cm) baking dish and set the dish in the oven. Pour hot water from the kettle into the baking dish until it reaches about halfway up the side of the springform pan. Bake for 25 to 28 minutes or until the top is golden brown and a cake tester inserted in the center comes out clean.

Carefully remove the springform pan from the baking dish and immediately place the cooled rice flour cake on top of the cheesecake soufflé, pressing down gently so it sticks. Let stand for about 4 minutes. Unclasp the springform pan and remove the ring of parchment paper. Let cool for 10 minutes, then place cake in the refrigerator for about 2 hours to set.

For the chèvre cheesecake mousse

In a large bowl, using an electric mixer, beat the heavy cream on high speed until stiff peaks form. Refrigerate until ready to use.

Fill a bowl with ice water, add the gelatin sheets, and let soak until softened. Remove the gelatin sheets from the ice water and squeeze out as much water as possible.

Set a medium bowl over a medium pot of simmering water. Add the crème fraîche, honey, and softened gelatin and whisk until melted and homogenous.

In the bowl of a stand mixer fitted with the paddle attachment, combine the cream cheese, chèvre, sugar, lemon zest and juice, and salt and beat on medium speed until light and fluffy. Stop the mixer, add the warm crème fraîche mixture, and mix on low speed for about 4 minutes or until incorporated with no lumps. If the mixture is lumpy, continue mixing for a few more minutes. Add ½ of the whipped cream and mix to lighten the texture then add the remaining whipped cream, gently folding until no streaks remain. Transfer to a resealable container and refrigerate for at least 1 hour or until ready to use.

For the assembly

Using the parchment paper overhang, transfer the cheesecake base consisting of the crust, soufflé, and rice cake layer to a 10-inch (25 cm) or larger cake plate (it will be easier if the plate is relatively flat) and quickly pull the paper out from underneath. Build the cake by piling the chèvre mousse on the cake from the crust up. Sculpt the mousse so that the peak comes to a sharp point.

Refrigerate the entire cake for at least 4 hours or until set then cut with a hot knife and serve.

Hugo Ortega

"America has been great to me. Many people don't even understand what is here.

First and foremost, the number one thing: opportunity. For me to be invited to the table, it's been a life change. So for me it's very simple to embrace responsibility. I want to do whatever it takes."

Hugo Ortega grew up on a mountaintop in Mexico, tending goats with his grandmother. At age fifteen he went to work in a Procter & Gamble factory in Mexico City, but he did not stay long. "In Mexico," he says, "we have a saying: 'If you're born poor, you'll die poor.' I wanted more from life."

In search of more, he headed north in 1984, to Houston, where he experienced homelessness before he found work as a dishwasher and began working two jobs at once. Soon he was hired away by Backstreet Cafe, whose owner, Tracy Vaught, promoted him to line cook, then sent him to culinary school. Upon graduation he returned as chef, putting the restaurant on the map. With Vaught, Ortega went on to open Hugo's, specializing in regional Mexican food, then Caracol, with a coastal emphasis, and, most recently, Xochi, centered on Oaxacan cuisine. The two married in 1994 and Ortega became a US citizen in 1996. Ortega was named Best Chef: Southwest by the James Beard Foundation in 2017; he won the title after six straight years as a finalist, becoming the first Mexican-born chef to do so. He is also a partner at Origen, in Oaxaca, and the author of two cookbooks.

Hugo Ortega

Squash Blossom Salad
(Ensalada de Flor de Calabaza)

For the past twenty-five years, I've been buying herbs from Fresh Herbs of Houston, which was founded by a Vietnamese woman named Pat, who came here back in the 1970s, and has been farming in Texas for many years. A decade ago, she asked me what special ingredients I might want for my menu and I answered *flor de calabaza* (squash blossoms). Pat has been growing squash blossoms for my restaurants ever since, and during the long summer season I buy more than a thousand of her blossoms each week. So, we two immigrants help each other.

In Mexico, especially in Puebla and Oaxaca, squash blossoms are a way of life. I put them in tamales and sauces, serve them the traditional way with blue corn and tortillas, and make them the star of this salad.

12 cherry tomatoes
3 cups (60 g) purslane florets
1 cup (60 g) frisée
10 squash blossoms, stems removed
8 zucchini ribbons (cut with a vegetable peeler or on a mandoline)
1 watermelon radish, thinly sliced
1 small beet, peeled and thinly sliced
3 tablespoons extra-virgin olive oil
3 tablespoons freshly squeezed lime juice
¼ teaspoon salt
¼ pound (110 g) fresh goat cheese, rolled into small balls

Heat a small saucepan over medium heat for 2 minutes. Add the cherry tomatoes and cook, swirling occasionally, for about 2 minutes or until the skins blister. Remove from the heat and let cool.

In a large bowl, toss together the purslane florets, frisée, 6 of the squash blossoms, the zucchini ribbons, watermelon radish, and beet.

In a small bowl, whisk together the extra-virgin olive oil, lime juice, and salt. Drizzle the dressing over the salad and gently toss to coat. Transfer the salad to a platter, garnish with the roasted tomatoes, goat cheese balls, and the remaining squash blossoms. Serve immediately.

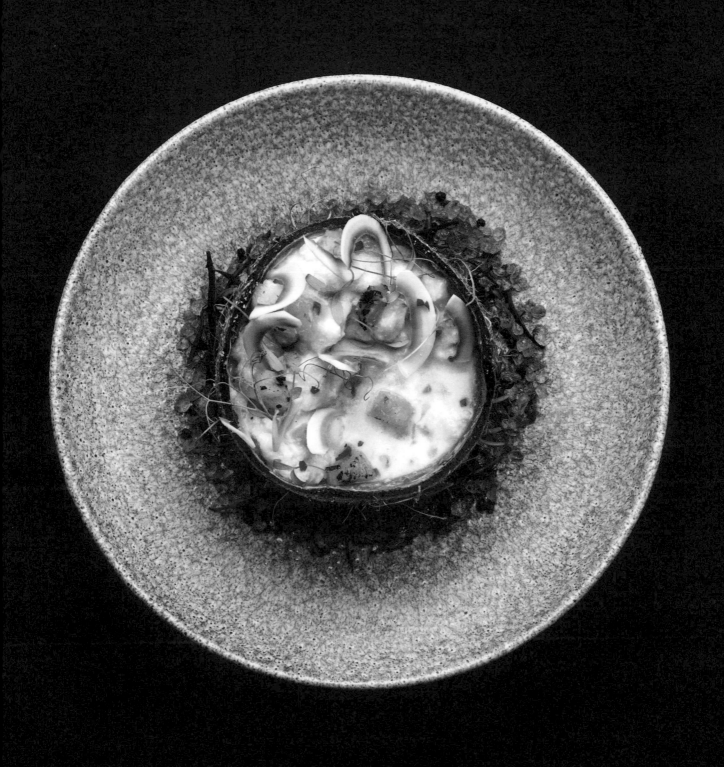

Hugo Ortega

Coconut Ceviche
(Ceviche de Coco)

Serves 4

Mexico has more than seven thousand miles of oceanfront and a wonderful coastal cuisine, especially along the Pacific. In comparison with other cultures, we add a lot of flavor to our fish dishes, so they're rich and spicy. With so many peppers, herbs, and charred onions and garlic, you could say we season our fish too much, but it works.

At the restaurant, we take the flesh and water from coconuts and reduce them into a sauce, which we serve with ceviche in a hard shell coconut. At home, you can use canned coconut cream instead of making your own.

At the restaurant, we also shave young coconut into chips, which we dry over the comal for a crunchy garnish, and combine rock salt with red beets to add a beautiful pink color, then everything is set atop seaweed for serving.

For the coconut cream
1 young coconut
1 mature coconut
Coconut water, as needed
Granulated sugar, to taste

For the ceviche
1 (3-ounce / 85-g) piece pineapple
1 large orange
¾ pound (340 g) skinless red
    snapper fillet, cut into cubes
1½ cups (360 ml) freshly squeezed
    lime juice
1 teaspoon salt
½ teaspoon finely diced fresh
    habañero chile, seeded first
    if desired
¾ cup (45 g) large unsweetened
    toasted coconut flakes
¼ cup (8 g) fresh cilantro leaves or
    sprouts
½ teaspoon extra-virgin olive oil

For the coconut cream
Using the bottom edge of a large knife, crack open the young coconut where the top naturally breaks from the shell. Pour the coconut water into a liquid measuring cup and set aside. Using a spoon, scrape the white flesh away from the coconut shell and remove any brown skin. Measure the amount of flesh then transfer to a medium saucepan.

To open the mature coconut, use a paring knife to puncture the coconut at the eyes. Pour the coconut water into the measuring cup with the coconut water from the young coconut. Using the dull side of a large knife, strike the coconut in several places at the circumference until the coconut splits in half. Pry the flesh away from the shell and remove any brown skin. Measure the amount of flesh then add ½ to the saucepan with the young coconut flesh, reserving the rest for another use.

Based on the amount of coconut flesh you measured, add an equal amount of coconut water, using the coconut water from the young and mature coconuts and adding purchased coconut water as needed. Cover and bring to a simmer over medium heat then reduce the heat to low and cook for 15 minutes. Remove from the heat and let cool to warm.

Pour the coconut flesh and liquid into a blender and purée. Add sugar to taste. Transfer to a container and let cool completely before using.

For the ceviche
Light a grill or preheat a grill pan over medium-high heat. Grill the pineapple, turning once, for 2 to 3 minutes per side or until grill marks appear. Let cool then chop into bite-size pieces.

Cut the orange peel and rind from the orange then use a small sharp knife to cut in between the membranes to release the orange segments into a small bowl.

In a bowl, cover the fish with the lime juice and let stand 10 minutes. Drain the fish, season to taste with salt, and mix well. Add 1 cup (240 ml) of the coconut cream, along with the grilled pineapple, orange segments, and habañero, and mix well to combine. Transfer to a platter or bowls, garnish with the coconut flakes and cilantro, drizzle with extra-virgin olive oil, and serve.

Laura and Sayat Ozyilmaz

Sayat and Laura Ozyilmaz, both chefs, are husband and wife.

Growing up in Chilpancingo, Mexico, Laura knew she wanted to be a chef. She studied at Ambrosía Centro Culinario in Mexico City, at the Culinary Institute of America in New York, and at the Basque Culinary Center in Spain. She has cooked at Mugaritz in Spain and at Café Boulud and Eleven Madison Park—which has been called the best restaurant in the world—in New York.

Sayat moved from Istanbul to the US on a full college scholarship to study molecular evolution. But when it was time to go to business school, he instead enrolled at the Culinary Institute of America. He went on to cook at the world-renowned Blue Hill at Stone Barns and Le Bernardin, both in New York.

Laura and Sayat met in New York and embarked on a trip across Mexico and the United States, cooking at two dozen prestigious restaurants including Pujol in Mexico City, Husk in Charleston, South Carolina, and Robuchon in New York. In San Francisco, they joined high-end kitchens but also began hosting their own pop-ups under the name Istanbul Modern SF. With sold-out events and long waiting lists, they embraced the pop-up full time and soon celebrated their 10,000th diner.

"We came here for a great education and decided to stay. Our American society is not perfect—and we now own up to its continued betterment—but for us both, the fact that hard work provided a clear path to self-actualization and success was the most important reason why we stayed.

Being immigrants not only defined our path but also set us apart."

Laura and Sayat Ozyilmaz

Turkish Eggs with Chickpeas and Garlic Labneh

Serves 4

Sayat has always had the vision to create a borderless cuisine that brings together all the cuisines of the Eastern Mediterranean. By paying respect to the many cultures that have left a mark on Istanbul, we tell a story of what could have been. Food is a unifying force and its cultural nuances should be appreciated and celebrated, and never used to keep us apart. We feel empowered to build our San Francisco dining community with this vision of a more cohesive Middle East.

For the tomato sauce
2 tablespoons olive oil
1 cup (125 g) finely chopped onion
2 cloves garlic, minced
1 tablespoon Turkish pepper paste
1 teapoon Urfa pepper flakes
1 tablespoon white miso
2 cups (360 g) large diced
    tomatoes
1 cup (185 g) dried chickpeas,
    soaked overnight
4 cups (960 ml) vegetable stock
Salt
½ cup (120 ml) pomegranate
    concentrate

For the garlic labneh
1 cup (240 ml) labneh
    (or Greek yogurt)
¼ cup (60 ml) water
1 tablespoon extra-virgin olive oil
1 clove garlic, finely grated
Salt

For za'atar breadcrumbs
3 tablespoons olive oil
½ cup (25 g) fresh breadcrumbs
1 tablespoon Palestinian za'atar,
    plus more to taste
1 teaspoon sumac, plus more to
    taste

For the eggs
4 large eggs

For the tomato sauce
In a small saucepan, heat the olive oil over medium heat. Add the onion and garlic in a single layer and cook, stirring occasionally, for about 6 minutes or until translucent. Add the pepper paste, pepper flakes, and white miso and stir until incorporated then lower the heat and cook for about 2 minutes or until the pepper paste is slightly browned. Add the tomatoes and bring to a simmer. Drain and rinse the chickpeas then add to the pot, along with the vegetable stock, and bring to a simmer. Continue simmering until the chickpeas start to soften then add the pomegranate concentrate and season to taste with salt.

Continue simmering until the chickpeas are fully cooked—you should be able to squash them between your fingers with no effort. While the chickpeas cook, make the garlic labneh.

For the garlic labneh
In a small bowl, whisk together the labneh, water, extra-virgin olive oil, and garlic and season to taste with salt.

For za'atar breadcrumbs
In a small skillet, heat the olive oil over medium-high heat. Add the breadcrumbs and cook, stirring, for about 3 minutes or until browned. Transfer to a paper towel to drain briefly then toss with the za'atar and sumac, adding more za'atar and sumac to taste.

For the eggs
Fill a large bowl with ice water and bring a medium saucepan of water to a boil. Add the eggs to the boiling water and simmer for 6 minutes then immediately transfer to the ice water and let cool. Once the eggs are cool enough to handle, peel and set aside.

Ladle the chickpea stew into 4 bowls then top with soft-boiled eggs, garlic labneh, and breadcrumbs and serve.

Laura and Sayat Ozyilmaz

Branzino Wrapped in Grape Leaves with Muhammara

Serves 2 to 4

It's been both easy and incredibly rewarding to connect with immigrants who have chosen a similar path. Through food and often with in-depth knowledge of our own cultural heritages, we have connected with and learned from our colleagues and now our employees. We have the warmest moments in our kitchens and restaurants, when we find the common threads between different cuisines. Many friends and family members have sacrificed for us to be here. We're building a restaurant and a community interwoven into our immigrant story.

For the muhammara
½ cup (120 ml) olive oil
½ medium onion, finely diced
4 cloves garlic, minced
½ teaspoon ground cumin
2 small red bell peppers, finely diced
3 tablespoons pomegranate concentrate
⅔ cup (80 g) toasted walnuts, roughly chopped
2 tablespoons freshly squeezed lemon juice
1 teaspoon Marash pepper flakes
Salt

For the walnut sauce
1 cup (100 g) toasted walnuts
2½ cups (600 ml) vegetable stock
2 tablespoons freshly squeezed lemon juice
1 teaspoon salt

For the branzino
2 whole branzino, about 1 pound (450 g) each
2 tablespoons olive oil
1 tablespoon minced garlic
2 teaspoons salt
6 cured grape leaves
1 lemon

For the muhammara
In a large skillet, heat the olive oil over medium high heat. Add the onion, garlic, and cumin and cook, stirring, for about 3 minutes or until the onions are translucent and the garlic is cooked through. Add the red bell peppers and pomegranate concentrate and cook for 10 to 12 minutes or until the water released by the peppers is completely evaporated. Stir in the toasted walnuts, lemon juice, and pepper flakes and season to taste with salt.

For the walnut sauce
In a food processor or blender, purée the toasted walnuts and vegetable stock for about 2 minutes or until the texture is silky. Add the lemon juice and salt and pulse to incorporate. Transfer to a small saucepan and heat gently over medium-low heat. Keep warm.

For the branzino
Preheat the oven to 425°F (220°C). Line a baking sheet with parchment paper and set a rack on top.
Rub the fish with the olive oil, garlic, and salt. Wrap the fish in the grape leaves and transfer to the rack on the baking sheet. Bake for 15 minutes or until the flesh easily pulls away from the backbone. Use a knife and fork to remove the grape leaves then squeeze the lemon over the fish and serve with muhammara and warm walnut sauce.

"As immigrants in the US, no matter what industry we're in, it's important that we are able to share our heritage, stand up for where we come from, and also feel free to express ourselves wherever we go, between different cuisines."

Argentina $\longrightarrow$ Brooklyn, New York

Norberto Piattoni

Argentinian-born Norberto Piattoni, who cooked for four years with the internationally famous chef Francis Mallmann, became known stateside for an impressive emulation of his mentor's open-fire cooking, in a restaurant called Metta in Brooklyn's Fort Greene. There, the tiny open kitchen uses no gas—instead, Piattoni cooked over wood and charcoal to create dazzling food with intense flavors, and not just of smoke.

Piattoni, who studied chemical engineering before turning to food, left Mallmann's El Garzón to immigrate to the US when he received a job offer in Kentucky. He went on to cook at the revolutionary Bar Tartine in San Francisco, where he picked up a second set of skills, focused on preserving and curing.

Piattoni's cuisine draws on his Argentine roots, but has expanded to take on American, Italian, and Asian accents. Flames from cherry and oak add flavor to the charred chili sauce and chimichurri-slathered steaks, but one standby is spared the heat: beef-heart carpaccio.

Norberto Piattoni

Grilled Whole Fish with Tomato-Fennel Sauce

Serves 4 to 8

I like to grill whole fish slowly so it stays juicy. I serve it with a Basque-style sauce of melted tomatoes and fennel, seasoned with paprika—you'll want to put it on everything.

2 tablespoons canola oil
1 large white onion, thinly sliced
1 fennel bulb, cut in half lengthwise, cored, and thinly sliced
6 cloves garlic, thinly sliced
4 tomatoes, cut into 1-inch (2.5 cm) cubes
1 teaspoon chili powder
½ teaspoon hot paprika
2 cups (480 ml) fish or chicken stock
5 teaspoons salt
1 large (4 to 6-pound / 1.8 to 2.7-kg) whole fish, such as black sea bass or snapper (or 4 small 1-pound / 450g whole fish, such as branzino) gutted and scaled
2 tablespoons grapeseed oil, plus more for the grill

In a medium saucepan, heat the canola oil over medium heat. Add the white onion, fennel, and garlic and cook, stirring often, for about 8 minutes or until the onion is translucent. Stir in the tomatoes, chili powder, and hot paprika. Reduce the heat to medium-low and simmer for 5 to 6 minutes or until the tomatoes are softened and slightly broken down. Stir in the fish or chicken stock, raise the heat to medium, and cook for about 10 minutes or until the sauce is reduced to about 3 cups (720 ml). Season with 1 teaspoon of the salt. Remove the sauce from the heat, cover, and keep warm.

Rinse the fish under cool running water then pat it dry with paper towels. Place on a large rimmed baking sheet, drizzle both sides with the grapeseed oil, and sprinkle all over with the remaining 4 teaspoons of salt.

Open the bottom and top vents of a charcoal grill completely. Fill 2 chimney starters with charcoal briquettes so they are completely full then light the briquettes. When the briquettes are covered with gray ash, pour them in an even layer on the bottom of the grill. (The internal temperature should be 375°F to 400°F / 190°C to 200°C.) Oil the grill grates with a little grapeseed oil.

Grill the fish, uncovered, for about 9 minutes for a large fish and 5 minutes for small fish or until the outside is charred and the meat on the bottom fillet pulls away from bones. Using 2 large fish spatulas, carefully flip the fish and grill, uncovered, for about 8 minutes for a large fish and 5 minutes for small fish or until the meat is opaque and flaky.

Using fish spatulas, carefully transfer the fish to a serving platter. Spoon the sauce over the fish and serve immediately.

Norberto Piattoni

Charred Sweet Potatoes with Elecampane Cream and Honey Gastrique

Serves 8

Coal-roasting sweet potatoes caramelizes their flesh while imparting a smoky aroma. We drizzle them with a honey-vinegar reduction called a gastrique, and serve them with whipped cream infused with musky, lightly bitter elecampane, a dried root used in homeopathic remedies. Elecampane is available online, but you can also make this recipe without it—the sweet potatoes will still be delicious. Look for the optional sweet potato leaves at farmers markets.

¼ cup (50 g) granulated sugar
1 tablespoon elecampane root pieces
½ teaspoon salt
1 cup (240 ml) heavy cream
8 sweet potatoes, about ¾ pound (340 g) each
¼ cup (60 ml) honey
¼ cup (60 ml) honey vinegar (or rice vinegar)
8 sweet potato leaves, for garnish (optional)
Bee pollen, for garnish (optional)

Preheat the oven to 350°F (180°C).

In a mini food processor, blend the sugar, elecampane root, and salt until finely chopped. Transfer the mixture to a small bowl then add the heavy cream and stir until the sugar is dissolved. Cover and refrigerate for 2 hours.

While the cream mixture is chilling, spread the sweet potatoes on a baking sheet and bake for 35 to 40 minutes or until just fork-tender.

In a small saucepan, bring the honey to a boil over medium heat and cook for about 3 minutes or until reduced by a quarter. Stir in the honey vinegar and cook, stirring occasionally, for 3 to 4 minutes or until the mixture is slightly reduced and syrupy. Let cool to room temperature then refrigerate until chilled.

Pour the chilled cream mixture through a fine-mesh strainer into a large bowl. Discard the solids. Using an electric mixer on medium-high speed, beat the cream for about 3 minutes or until soft peaks form. Cover and refrigerate until ready to serve.

Open the bottom and top vents of a charcoal grill completely. Fill 2 chimney starters with charcoal briquettes so they are completely full then light the briquettes. When the briquettes are covered with gray ash, pour them in an even layer on the bottom of the grill. (The internal temperature should be 375°F to 400°F / 190°C to 200°C.)

Using tongs, nestle the baked sweet potatoes in the coals and roast for 15 to 20 minutes or until the sweet potatoes are cooked through and the skins are charred. Transfer to a baking sheet and let stand until cool enough to handle. Brush away any ashes with a paper towel then slice the sweet potatoes about ¾-inch thick (2 cm) and divide among 8 shallow bowls. Dollop 2 tablespoons of the whipped cream next to the sweet potatoes in each bowl then drizzle with the honey gastrique. Garnish each bowl with a sweet potato leaf and a pinch of bee pollen, if using.

Ethiopia and Sweden ⟶ New York, New York

Marcus Samuelsson

Marcus Samuelsson's journey has been remarkable. As a young child in Ethiopia, he lost his mother to tuberculosis. Violence and famine plagued the country. Samuelsson and his sister were adopted by a family in Sweden.

One of Samuelsson's earliest Swedish memories is of standing in front of their fridge. "We'd been underfed in Ethiopia, and the idea that food could just come out of this door was such a big deal to us," he recalls. He soon learned that the bounty was the result of a long process of preserving and cooking—often by his new grandmother, Helga.

She put him to work picking blueberries and rhubarb, pickling lingonberries and mushrooms, and catching and preserving fish. She also taught him to make bread, meatballs, and other Swedish staples from scratch. These early lessons formed the foundation for Samuelsson's success as a chef.

By eighteen, Samuelsson landed his first culinary scholarship, which led to opportunities in Japan, Switzerland, and France. Next, he set out for the US, where he says the "possibility of diversity" is most vital. In New York, Samuelsson became executive chef of Aquavit and the youngest chef ever to receive a three-star review from the *New York Times*. In 2003, the James Beard Foundation named him Best Chef: New York City; soon after, he began winning television cooking shows. He oversaw the Obama administration's first state dinner, wrote a bestselling memoir, *Yes, Chef*, and opened restaurants in New York, Montreal, Bermuda, London, and beyond.

When Red Rooster, his most famous restaurant, opened in Harlem in 2011, it was hailed by the *Times* as a "real stride forward" for the neighborhood and for New York. "'Restaurant' means to restore your community," Samuelsson says. "When I think about the 180 employees of Red Rooster, I know we're doing that." Samuelsson runs the Harlem EatUp! Festival, serves on the board of City Harvest, and co-chairs the Careers through Culinary Arts Program. He hosts a PBS series, *No Passport Required*, which celebrates immigrants' contributions to American food and culture. He is the winner of the 2019 Vilcek Prize in Culinary Arts.

"Being an immigrant in the US means being American. Unless we're Native Americans, we're all immigrants. That's what makes this such a beautiful country."

Marcus Samuelsson

Helga's Meatballs with Gravy

Serves 4

Growing up and cooking with my grandmother, I never thought that what I learned in her kitchen would someday be trendy. But for the last ten years, restaurant cooking has been all about comfort food, including burgers, fried chicken, and meatballs. This recipe comes from my Swedish grandmother, so it is both a culinary heirloom and a reflection of Sweden, where meatballs are sold from kiosks with mashed potatoes. I like to serve the meatballs over a carrot-apple-potato mash, with pickled red onions, but plain mashed potatoes are also delicious. It's wonderful on a cold fall or winter day.

For the meatballs
2 tablespoons olive oil
1 medium red onion, finely
    chopped
½ cup (70 g) dry breadcrumbs
¼ cup (60 ml) heavy cream
½ pound (225 g) ground chuck
    or sirloin
½ pound (225 g) ground veal
½ pound (225 g) ground pork
2 tablespoons honey
1 large egg
Salt and freshly ground pepper
Canola oil

For the gravy
1 cup (240 ml) chicken broth
½ cup (120 ml) heavy cream
¼ cup (60 ml) lingonberry
    preserves
2 tablespoons juice from pickled
    cucumbers
Salt and freshly ground pepper

For the meatballs
In a small skillet, heat the olive oil over medium heat until shimmering. Add the red onion and cook for about 5 minutes or until softened. Remove from the heat and let cool.

In a large bowl, combine the breadcrumbs and heavy cream, stirring with a fork, until the crumbs are moistened. Add the sautéed onion, the beef, veal, pork, honey, and egg and season to taste with salt and pepper. Moisten your hands and mix until well combined. Form the mixture into 24 roughly golf ball–sized meatballs and transfer to a plate moistened with water.

Lightly oil a grill pan with canola oil and heat over medium-high heat. Working in batches, grill the meatballs, turning occasionally, for about 5 minutes or until browned all over and cooked through. Season to taste with salt and pepper and cook the remaining meatballs. Keep warm.

For the gravy
In a large saucepan, combine the chicken broth, heavy cream, lingonberry preserves, and pickle juice and bring to a simmer over medium-high heat. Add the meatballs, reduce the heat to medium, and simmer for about 5 minutes or until the gravy thickens slightly and the meatballs are heated through. Season to taste with salt and pepper and serve.

Marcus Samuelsson

Berbere-Smoked Salmon with Sweet Potato Waffles

Serves 4

This salmon is cold-smoked at home using cherry smoke wood sticks from Shinsei Sangyo, which are available online. You can use wood chips instead, but they burn at a faster rate, so you must smoke the salmon in three-minute increments and remove it from the heat so it doesn't cook.

Mitmita is an Ethiopian spice blend that contains bird's eye chili, cardamom, cloves, and sometimes other sweet spices.

For the salmon
4¼ cups (1 liter) water
1¾ cups (350 g) granulated sugar
1¾ cups (350 g) kosher salt
1 (1-pound / 450-g) skinless salmon fillet
1 teaspoon white miso
½ teaspoon honey
½ teaspoon soy sauce
2 to 3 teaspoons berbere spice
1 (1-inch / 2.5-cm) piece Japanese cherry smoke wood stick

For the waffles
1 large sweet potato, peeled and quartered
2 cups (260 g) all-purpose flour
2 tablespoons plus 2 teaspoons granulated sugar
1 teaspoon salt
2½ teaspoons baking powder
1 teaspoon baking soda
1 tablespoon ground cinnamon
1 teaspoon ground nutmeg
1 teaspoon ground ginger
¼ teaspoon ground allspice
2 large eggs
1 cup (240 ml) buttermilk
¼ cup (60 g) unsalted butter, melted
Canola oil or nonstick cooking spray, for the waffle iron

For serving
⅔ cup (150 ml) honey
1½ teaspoons mitmita
Fresh greens and dill sprigs, for garnish
4 poached eggs (optional)

For the salmon
In a large pot, bring the 4¼ cups (1 liter) water to a boil. Add the sugar and salt and stir to dissolve. Chill over an ice bath or refrigerate until cold.

Once the brine is cold, add the salmon and soak for 30 minutes then drain well.

Place the smoke stick in a roasting pan and set a rack on top. Ignite the stick and when it starts to smoke, arrange the salmon on the rack but not directly over the stick. Cover the pan tightly with foil and allow the fish to smoke for about 20 minutes. Uncover the fish and pour water on the stick so it stops smoking.

In a small bowl, mix together the miso, honey, and soy sauce. Spread the berbere spice on a plate. Brush the miso mixture all over the salmon then roll the fish in the berbere spice and set aside.

Continued ⟶

Marcus Samuelsson

For the waffles

In a small saucepan, cover the sweet potato with cold water and bring to a boil over medium-high heat. Continue boiling for 15 to 20 minutes or until very soft. Drain the sweet potato, transfer to a food processor, and let cool to warm. Purée the sweet potato until smooth then measure 1 cup (240 g) and reserve the rest for another use.

Heat a waffle iron.

In a large bowl, whisk together the flour, sugar, salt, baking powder, baking soda, cinnamon, nutmeg, ginger, and allspice.

In a medium bowl, whisk together the eggs, buttermilk, and the 1 cup (240 g) sweet potato purée. Add to the flour mixture and stir together. Add the melted butter and mix until incorporated.

Preheat the oven to 200°F (100°C) and set a baking sheet in the oven.

Oil or spray a Belgian waffle iron as needed. Scoop about ¾ cup (180 ml) of the waffle batter (or whatever amount is suggested by the manufacturer's instructions) into the iron and cook according to the manufacturer's instructions. As the waffles are done, transfer them to the baking sheet in the oven to keep warm. Repeat with the remaining batter. (Any leftover waffles can be frozen on a baking sheet and then stored in a resealable bag in the freezer for up to 1 month; reheat in a 350°F/180°C oven or a toaster oven.)

For serving

In a small bowl, mix together the honey and mitmita.

Thickly slice the smoked salmon. Transfer the warm waffles to plates then arrange the smoked salmon alongside, drizzle with some of the mitmita honey, and garnish with fresh dill and greens. Serve with the remaining honey and, optionally, a poached egg on top.

South Korea ⟶ Philadelphia, Pennsylvania

Peter Serpico

Born in Seoul, South Korea, Peter Serpico was adopted at age two and raised in Maryland. Growing up on lasagna, manicotti, and apple pie, Serpico saw that food has the power to bring people together, and he set his sights on a serious culinary career.

After graduating from the Baltimore International College Culinary School, Serpico moved to New York and began cooking at Bouley, then Sumile and Jovia, mastering the technique and temperament that would take him to some of the top kitchens in the country.

In 2006, Serpico began working with David Chang as sous chef at the original Momofuku Noodle Shop in the East Village. For the next six years, Serpico worked with Chang to open Momofuku Ssäm Bar, Momofuku Ko (where he was the opening chef de cuisine), Má Pêche, and ultimately, Momofuku Sydney, helping to grow the family of restaurants while maintaining the highest level of quality in each location. As director of culinary operations for Momofuku, Serpico was central to menu creation and execution at all the restaurants, and earned three stars from the *New York Times*, a James Beard Award, and two Michelin Stars, among other accolades.

In 2012, Serpico met Philadelphia restaurateur Stephen Starr, whose STARR Restaurants group operates dozens of establishments. The two formed a collaboration and Serpico opened his eponymous upscale restaurant in Philadelphia in 2013. It has received critical acclaim from outlets including *Food & Wine*, *Travel + Leisure*, and the *Washington Post*, as well as a glowing "Three Bell" review from the *Philadelphia Inquirer*.

"American food is always evolving. There has been a great shift and food is becoming part of our culture, much like it has been for other countries for hundreds of years.

America means opportunity for immigrants. The opportunity to be successful seems even more possible today, no matter where you come from. Power and influence have been dispersed. Everyone seems to be on a more even playing field, which is most important to immigrants and their families."

Peter Serpico

Steamed Egg Custard

Serves 4

I based this recipe on chawan mushi. The first time I had the classic Japanese egg custard I was blown away by the texture. There is something that feels so nurturing and heartwarming about this dish. I think it's perfect as is, but you can add or subtract ingredients to make it your own.

2 cups (480 ml) chicken stock
3 large eggs
1 teaspoon soy sauce
1 teaspoon salt
12 extra-jumbo (16/20 count) shrimp, peeled, deveined, and minced
1 clove garlic, sliced
1 scallion, sliced
3 ounces (85 g) enoki mushrooms, cut into 1-inch (2.5 cm) pieces
12 shiitake mushrooms, stems removed and caps sliced
16 fresh flat-leaf parsley leaves

In a medium bowl, whisk together the chicken stock, eggs, soy sauce, and salt.

Divide the shrimp, garlic, scallion, enoki and shiitake mushrooms, and the parsley leaves between 4 small bowls, ramekins, or handle-free coffee cups. Divide the egg mixture among the 4 bowls and wrap each one in plastic wrap.

Set up a steamer pot or arrange a bamboo steamer over a wok. (Alternatively, arrange a round rack or a flat bowl in the bottom of a deep skillet with a lid.) Fill the pot or wok with 1 to 2 inches (2.5 to 5 cm) of water, making sure the water does not come into direct contact with the steaming rack or bamboo steamer. Bring the water to a boil then reduce the heat to low. Carefully set the bowls filled with the egg mixture on the steaming rack or in the steamer, cover, and slowly steam for about 15 minutes or until the custard is just set but still wobbles in the center. Carefully unwrap the custards and enjoy.

Peter Serpico

Korean Sweet Pastry (Hoetteok)

This is a popular Korean street food in winter. It's often made with ground nuts like walnuts and almonds, but here I use shredded coconut with cinnamon and light brown sugar.

For the dough
1 teaspoon instant yeast
1 teaspoon granulated sugar
½ cup (120 ml) whole milk, lukewarm
1 cup (130 g) all-purpose flour
½ teaspoon salt
2 tablespoons canola oil

For the filling
⅓ cup (65 g) light brown sugar
¼ cup (20 g) shredded unsweetened coconut
1 tablespoon maple syrup
½ teaspoon ground cinnamon
Salt

For the dough
In a small bowl, stir together the yeast, granulated sugar, and lukewarm milk and let stand 5 minutes. In the bowl of a stand mixer fitted with the dough hook attachment, whisk together the flour and salt. Add the yeast mixture and mix with the hook just until incorporated. Cover and let rest for 1 to 2 hours or until doubled in size.

For the filling
In a small bowl, mix together the light brown sugar, shredded coconut, maple syrup, cinnamon, and a pinch of salt.

Punch down the dough then use scissors to cut it into 4 equal pieces. Lightly dust your hands with flour and roll each piece of dough into a ball that's roughly the size of a golf ball. Lightly stretch each ball into a small pancake about the size of your hand. Working with 1 pancake at a time, place ¼ of the filling in the center and pull the sides up and around to enclose the filling then shape it into a ball with the filling completely tucked inside. Repeat to make 3 more balls.

In a large skillet, heat the canola oil over medium heat. Add the pastry balls and cook, pressing lightly with a spatula, for 2 to 3 minutes or until browned on the bottom. Flip and cook, again pressing lightly with a spatula, for 2 to 3 minutes or until browned on the other side. Serve hot.

Israel ⟶ New Orleans, Louisiana

Alon Shaya

Alon Shaya says cooking has been essential to his survival.

His family immigrated to Philadelphia when he was four, and it wasn't easy. But when his grandparents visited from Israel, the kitchen aromas of peppers and eggplant became his reconnection to feelings of family, love, and knowing who he was.

Cooking always came naturally—and centered his identity. In second grade, he presented his first cooking demonstration: spinach borekas. By high school, he wasn't taking life seriously, when his home economics teacher Donna Barnett saw his talent, became his mentor, showed him fine Philadelphia dining, and pointed him towards culinary school. He never looked back. After attending the Culinary Institute of America, he moved to Italy to master traditional technique and then to New Orleans where his dishes started winning attention and awards.

He was known for elevated Italian menus when a 2011 trip to Israel changed everything. "I started connecting with where my family came from, and who I was," he recalls.

Inspired by Israel, he began researching and recreating his grandmother's recipes and was soon putting Israeli riffs on his menu—like shakshuka, buttermilk biscuits with zataar, and a cauliflower-feta dish that sold 700 servings a week. Over time, as he embraced his cultural heritage at the stove, he forged new flavor combinations drawn from three cuisines: Italian, Israeli, and the American South.

Shaya now has been nominated for five James Beard Awards. In 2015, the foundation named him Best Chef: South, and *Southern Living* called him one of the 50 People Who Are Changing the South. The Beard Foundation named his restaurant, Shaya, Best New Restaurant the following year.

In 2016, Shaya joined forces with Barnett, his former home economics teacher, to start the Shaya Barnett Foundation, providing culinary education to high school students. He also published *Shaya: An Odyssey of Food, My Journey Back to Israel*. Part memoir and part cookbook, it shares his personal journey and explores the transformative power of food and cooking.

"Being an immigrant myself, I've always loved that my dreams in America could come true if I worked hard. My mother and father had to struggle—as being adults when they immigrated—so I could have a leg up and get an early start. Our story is the American Dream."

Alon Shaya

Israeli Couscous with Summer Vegetables and Caramelized Tomato

Serves 4 to 6

Hurricane Katrina happened at the end of August, a moment when a bounty of summer vegetables was available as we landed in North Carolina after evacuating New Orleans. This dish capitalizes on them with all the nourishment of comfort food, the kind of thing we sorely needed at that time. Toasting the tomato paste, as my *safta* (grandmother) taught me, adds a complex sweet-savory flavor—that one little technique is a trusted friend that I've relied upon through the years. Ingrained in my muscle memory and etched into my cooking, it made me feel she was with us in the kitchen during that crazy time.

Salt
1 large eggplant, stemmed and cut into 1-inch (2.5 cm) pieces
1 large zucchini, trimmed and cut into 1-inch (2.5 cm) pieces
1 yellow onion, chopped
½ cup (120 ml) olive oil
1 cup (150 g) Israeli couscous
4 sprigs fresh thyme
1 cup (30 g) fresh flat-leaf parsley leaves
3 cloves garlic, thinly sliced
¾ cup (200 g) tomato paste
½ cup (75 g) assorted pitted black or green olives, cut in half
8 fresh basil leaves, torn

Preheat the broiler to high.

In a large pot, combine 4 quarts (3.8 liters) of water and 1 tablespoon of salt and bring to a boil.

Meanwhile, in a large bowl, toss the eggplant, zucchini, and onion with ¼ cup (60 ml) of the olive oil, and 1 tablespoon of salt. Spread everything in an even layer on a baking sheet, and broil, stirring every 5 minutes, for 10 to 15 minutes or until the vegetables are evenly golden and the eggplant is very tender.

Once the water comes to a boil, add the couscous, and cook for about 6 minutes or until it's tender but still has a little bite. Drain.

Strip the leaves from the thyme and finely chop them with the parsley.

In a large skillet, warm the remaining ¼ cup (60 ml) of olive oil over medium heat. Add the garlic, thyme, and parsley and cook for 30 seconds to 1 minute or just until fragrant. Stir in the tomato paste, and cook, breaking it up with your spoon and reducing the heat as needed if the paste is browning too fast, for 5 to 10 minutes or until the paste is very fragrant and deeply caramelized. Remove the skillet from the heat then stir in the broiled vegetables and couscous, along with ½ cup (120 ml) of water. Season to taste with salt if needed. Fold in the olives and basil and serve warm. The couscous and vegetables can be made ahead and kept in an airtight container in the refrigerator overnight. Wait to add the basil and serve at room temperature.

Israel ⟶ Philadelphia, Pennsylvania

Michael Solomonov

Michael Solomonov was raised in Pittsburgh and returned to Israel at eighteen, where he found work in a bakery and began a world-changing culinary career. Bursting onto the Philadelphia food scene, he opened his groundbreaking restaurant Zahav just as the financial crisis hit. Undeterred, Solomonov white-knuckled his way to Zahav being widely named one of the best new restaurants of 2008, and to receiving a James Beard Award for the restaurant's cookbook of the same name. His modern Israeli haute cuisine highlights innovative interpretations of traditional foods: the apples and honey on Rosh Hashanah appear in a sesame pastilla with foie gras and caramelized onions, while the Chanukah sufganiyot is filled with Meyer lemon curd and cranberries.

Solomonov overcame addiction and was named the James Beard Foundation's Outstanding American Chef of 2017 (colloquially known as best chef in the country). In 2019, Zahav won the James Beard Award for Outstanding Restaurant. His cooking has been hailed in the *New York Times, Bon Appétit, Food & Wine, Esquire, Travel & Leisure* and many more. Beyond Zahav, his category-defying Israeli and Jewish flavors spawned a number of hummusiyas, delis, and falafel eateries in Philadelphia and beyond.

The internationally-known chef is also committed to his community, spearheading such projects as the Rooster Deli partnership with Broad Street Ministry, which feeds thousands of three-course meals to the city's most vulnerable residents every year.

"America was founded on the culture of immigration, which is now so ingrained in our country that our economy is even built on the work ethic and the culture of immigrants. That's the beauty of it. It's created necessary diversity."

Michael Solomonov

My Mom's Coffee-Braised Brisket

Serves 8

This is my take on the dish my mother served at virtually every special-occasion dinner of my childhood. And my mom's version was her take on the dish that her mother made. Brisket has a long history on the Jewish table, primarily because it was a very economical cut. When cooked properly, it's one of the most flavorful pieces of meat you can find. Whether it's first or second cut (the flat or the point) matters less than making sure the meat has a nice layer of fat on one side.

My grandmother made her brisket with carrots, potatoes, and Heinz chili sauce, which gave a traditional sweet-and-sour flavor. My mother added coffee—its deep, roasted flavors work well with beef. I add cardamom to evoke Turkish coffee, and I replace the sweetness of that chili sauce with dried apricots. You'll find braised eggs like the ones in this dish in cholent, or *hamin*, the Sabbath stew that is cooked slowly overnight and served on Saturday afternoon. They take on an almost creamy texture, and as the coffee braising liquid penetrates the shells, it colors the eggs and subtly flavors them. I finish the dish with grated horseradish for a little bit of pungency to wake up the long-cooked flavors.

2 tablespoons finely ground coffee
1½ tablespoons ground cardamom
1½ tablespoons ground black cardamom
1 tablespoon plus 1 teaspoon salt
1 brisket, first cut, about 4 pounds (1.8 kg)
¼ cup (60 ml) canola oil
2 large onions, sliced
4 carrots, sliced
10 cloves garlic, sliced
⅓ cup (75 ml) tomato paste
1½ cups (265 g) dried apricots
2 cups (480 ml) brewed coffee
8 large eggs in their shells
Grated fresh horseradish

In a small bowl, mix the ground coffee, cardamom, black cardamom, and salt and rub it into the brisket. Cover loosely with plastic wrap and refrigerate overnight.

Preheat the oven to 475°F (250°C) and set a rack inside a roasting pan.

Put the brisket on the rack and roast for about 20 minutes or until the exterior has browned. Remove the roasting pan from the oven, set the brisket aside, and remove the rack from the pan. Lower the oven temperature to 300°F (150°C).

In a large skillet, warm the canola oil over medium heat and add the onions, carrots, and garlic. Cook, stirring occasionally, for about 8 minutes or until the vegetables have softened but not browned. Add the tomato paste and cook for about 2 minutes or until it reduces slightly.

Transfer the vegetable mixture to the roasting pan without the rack. Return the brisket to the roasting pan then add the dried apricots, brewed coffee, and eggs in their shells. Add enough water to bring the liquid halfway up the side of the brisket. Cover the pan tightly with 2 layers of foil, return to the oven, and braise for 1 hour. Remove the eggs, gently tap them all over to make a network of small cracks, and return them to the roasting pan. Continue braising for about 3 hours or until the brisket shreds easily with a fork. Let the brisket cool in its braising liquid then refrigerate overnight.

When ready to serve, preheat the oven to 350°F (180°C). Slice the cold brisket, return it to the braising liquid, and bake for about 30 minutes or until warmed through. Spoon the broth over the meat. Serve with the peeled eggs and grated fresh horseradish.

Michael Solomonov

Feta Borekas

I was eighteen when I returned to Israel. One morning, as I walked past a bakery with display cases piled high with *borekas*, I asked for a job in broken Hebrew. I was told to show up the next day.

We made borekas in batches so large that it took four of us to lift the dough. I enjoyed the camaraderie. It is the exact feeling I still get after a busy night at Zahav—a sense of pride in myself and in the cooks who stand with me shoulder to shoulder. Most of them have made incredible sacrifices to come to this country, all to make a better life for their children. It is the story of America, and it is the story of Israel and of my grandparents, too.

For the dough
6½ cups (845 g) all-purpose flour
2 tablespoons kosher salt
¼ cup (60 ml) distilled
   white vinegar
2⅓ cups (555 ml) seltzer water
1½ cups plus 6 tablespoons (430 g)
   unsalted butter, softened

For the filling and assembly
10 ounces (280 g) crumbled feta
2 large eggs
2 tablespoons sesame seeds

For the dough
In the bowl of a stand mixer fitted with the paddle attachment, combine the flour, kosher salt, and distilled white vinegar. Mix on low while adding the seltzer in a slow, steady stream. Continue mixing for about 2 minutes or until the dough begins to pull away from the sides and bottom of the mixer.

On a floured work surface, knead the dough by hand for about 1 minute or just until it feels smooth and homogenous. Cover with a clean cotton cloth and let rest for 30 minutes.

Working with a floured rolling pin, roll out the dough to a roughly ¼-inch-thick (0.5 cm) rectangle with a long side facing you. (It should be at least 20 x 15 inches / 50 x 38 cm). Spread ½ the butter evenly across the middle third of the dough rectangle.

Fold the left third of the dough over the butter then fold the right third over the left third (they'll overlap). Fold the top and bottom edges toward the center the same way, forming a square. Wrap tightly with plastic wrap and refrigerate overnight.

On a floured work surface, arrange the dough square so that it's turned 90 degrees from the first time you folded it (that is, with the folded ends on the sides). Roll the chilled dough out to a ¼-inch-thick (0.5 cm) rectangle (again, about 20 x 15 inches / 50 x 38 cm). Spread the remaining butter evenly across the middle third of the rectangle. Fold the sides over the butter, and fold the top and bottom toward the center, forming a square. Wrap tightly with plastic wrap and refrigerate overnight.

On a floured work surface, arrange the dough square so that it's turned 90 degrees from the last fold and roll the chilled dough out to a ¼-inch-thick (0.5 cm) rectangle. Repeat the folding process, folding the sides into the center and then folding the top and bottom toward the center to make a square. (This time, don't add more butter.) Wrap tightly with plastic wrap and refrigerate overnight.

The next day, divide the dough into 3 equal pieces and set 1 aside for immediate use. The rest can be frozen for later. Roll the piece you are using into a 10 x 15-inch (25 x 38 cm) sheet. Make sure to keep the dough cold at all times (except when you're working with it).

For the filling and assembly
In a medium bowl, combine the feta with 1 of the eggs and stir well to combine.

Place the cold sheet of boreka dough on a floured work surface. Cut the dough into 8 (4-inch / 10-cm) squares. Spread about 2 heaping tablespoons of the feta filling onto half of a square of dough, leaving a roughly ½-inch (1.25 cm) border around the edge. Fold the dough over to form a rectangle and press at the edges to seal. Repeat until all the borekas are formed. Arrange on a parchment-lined baking sheet and refrigerate for 1 hour—the borekas should be cold and firm to the touch.

Preheat the oven to 425°F (220°C) and set a rack in the upper position.

Beat the remaining 1 egg and brush on the tops of the borekas then sprinkle with the sesame seeds and bake for about 15 minutes or until the dough is golden brown.

Covered, at room temperature, borekas will keep for 2 days. Don't refrigerate them. They'll reheat quickly and well in a 325°F (160°C) oven for 5 minutes. Filled borekas can be frozen before baking. In that case, put them directly in a preheated 425°F (220°) oven; don't thaw them first.

Mutsuko Soma

Mutsuko Soma was born and raised in Tochigi, Japan and came to the Pacific Northwest to attend the Art Institute of Seattle. After studying the culinary arts, she cooked in French, Spanish, and Japanese kitchens in Seattle, including the Harvest Vine and Saito's, and gained attention as a young executive chef at Chez Shea.

Soma moved back to Japan to care for her aging grandmother and was there when the catastrophic tsunami struck in 2011. During the destruction that followed, her US visa expired. Soma used these hardships as a time to master the art of soba making under her grandmother's expert guidance. While studying soba, Soma discovered that much of the buckwheat used in Japan is grown in Washington, one of the largest buckwheat producing states in the US. This reaffirmed her decision to introduce her soba to the Pacific Northwest.

Upon returning to Washington state, she began working with locally grown buckwheat and hosted soba pop-ups in Los Angeles and Seattle, which quickly gained attention. She now serves her nutty, toasty, hand-made soba through her restaurant, Kamonegi.

Recognized as a semifinalist for the James Beard Foundation's Best Chef: Northwest award and as Chef of the Year by Eater Seattle, Soma is also certified as a sake sommelier by the Japan Sommelier Association.

"I came to America to study the culinary arts, particularly European culinary arts. Throughout this time, I harbored an unspoken goal of bringing to the United States a traditional Japanese culinary tradition: soba. This journey began as a goal to introduce something new to a different audience, and it led to a personal journey and increased desire to inspire others through food and service."

Mutsuko Soma

Chicken Kara Age

This Japanese fried chicken is marinated before cooking for maximum flavor. Kitchen scissors make easy work of cutting the skin-on chicken into small pieces. If you can't find boneless skin-on thighs, use boneless, skinless thighs instead.

1 pound (450 g) boneless, skin-on chicken thighs, cut into 1- to 2-inch (2.5 to 5 cm) pieces
2 cloves garlic, minced
1 (1-inch / 2.5-cm) piece fresh ginger, minced
3 tablespoons soy sauce
2 tablespoons sake
Freshly ground pepper
Canola oil, for frying
1 large egg, lightly beaten
3 tablespoons cornstarch
2 tablespoons all-purpose flour
Shichimi togarashi (Japanese seven spice seasoning) and thinly sliced scallions, for garnish (optional)

In a large bowl, toss the chicken, garlic, ginger, soy sauce, sake, and a pinch of pepper then cover and refrigerate for 30 minutes to 24 hours.

In a large, deep pan, Dutch oven, or deep fryer, bring about 1 inch (2.5 cm) of canola oil to 325°F (160°C). Drain the marinade from the bowl of chicken then add the lightly beaten egg and toss to coat the chicken in the egg.

In a shallow bowl, mix the cornstarch and flour.

Set a rack over a baking sheet and arrange it near the stove. Working in batches as needed, toss the chicken in the cornstarch mixture until completely coated then carefully add the chicken to the hot oil and fry, turning occasionally, for about 8 minutes or until golden. Using a slotted spoon or a strainer with a handle, transfer the chicken to the rack and let cool slightly. Repeat to fry the remaining chicken.

For an extra-crispy exterior, you can double-fry the chicken: Increase the oil temperature to 375°F (190°C) then add the fried chicken and fry for about 3 minutes or until deep golden brown.

Let the chicken rest 5 minutes then garnish with shichimi togarashi and sliced scallions, if using, and serve.

Mutsuko Soma

Pork Miso Soup (Tonjiru)

This miso broth is wonderfully simple—it's just miso, sake, and water—but with tofu, pork, and vegetables, plus a garnish of shichimi togarashi and scallions, the finished soup makes a filling meal.

1 tablespoon toasted sesame oil
½ pound (225 g) pork butt, thinly sliced
2 ounces (60 g) diced daikon radish
2 ounces (60 g) diced carrot
2 ounces (60 g) sliced burdock root (or parsnip)
2 tablespoons sake
6 cups (1.4 liters) water
1 (14-ounce / 400 g) package medium tofu, diced
¼ cup (65 g) white miso
Shichimi togarashi (Japanese seven spice seasoning) and thinly sliced scallions (optional), for garnish

In a large, heavy-bottomed pot, heat the toasted sesame oil over medium heat. Add the pork and cook, stirring, for about 5 minutes or until nearly cooked through. Add the daikon radish, carrot, and burdock root and cook, stirring, for about 2 minutes or until the vegetables just start sizzling. Add the sake and water and bring to simmer. Reduce the heat to low and cook for about 20 minutes or until the vegetables are tender. Stir in the tofu and miso and bring just to a boil, then immediately remove from the heat.

Ladle the soup into cups or bowls, garnish with the shichimi togarashi and scallions, if using, and serve.

Daniela Soto-Innes

"I always wanted to be like my mom. Her dream was to become a chef, but back then in Mexico being a chef was not the most respected profession so she became a lawyer instead of following her dreams.

When we moved to the US I missed everything about Mexico, especially the food. Now I thank my mother for moving to this world full of amazing opportunities, this world where if you really care and push forward, anything is possible.

I knew that I needed to represent my roots and I had a responsibility as an immigrant to teach people about how beautiful and elegant my culture was.

Living in New York, running two of the busiest restaurants in the city, being a woman and on top of that being Mexican, has destroyed every single space of doubt I ever thought of something not possible."

The daughter of two lawyers, Daniela Soto-Innes emigrated from Mexico City to Texas at age twelve and was already working in kitchens at fourteen, having lied about her age to get in the door. After training at Le Cordon Bleu and cooking in New York and Europe, she returned to Mexico City with a stint at Pujol, Chef Enrique Olvera's world-renowned temple of modern Mexican cuisine. She was soon offered a full-time position working alongside Olvera, who is widely regarded as one of the best chefs in the world.

When Olvera was ready to open his first restaurant in the US, Cosme, he chose Soto-Innes to be its opening chef—at the age of twenty-three. She quickly won the James Beard Foundation's Rising Chef of the Year award, and Cosme earned a place on the World's 50 Best Restaurants list of 2017.

Cosme's high-end dishes feature Mexican foods with innovative interpretations, like the signature husk meringues with corn, and the cobia al pastor with puréed pineapple. Comfort foods like tonka bean and pecan atole and steaming, crispy churros give the menu popular appeal as well as critical acclaim. "I had a responsibility as an immigrant to teach people about how beautiful and elegant my culture was," says Soto-Innes. Her modern take on Mexican dining has drawn legions of fans, including President Obama, who ordered the duck carnitas.

Daniela Soto-Innes

Sea Buckthorn Aguachile with Kampachi and Cucumber Salsa

Serves 6

Aguachile is a type of Mexican ceviche, made here with Kampachi, a yellowtail tuna from Hawaii—you can use any sushi-grade tuna. Sour sea buckthorn berries grow on coastal and subalpine regions. Look for them at health food stores or online.

For the fish fumet base
¼ pound (110 g) fresh ginger, roughly chopped
1 small red onion, roughly chopped
1 clove garlic, roughly chopped
2 ounces (60 g) lemongrass, roughly chopped
1 ounce (28 g) celery, roughly chopped
½ ounce (15 g) fresh habañeros, seeded and roughly chopped
1 cup (240 ml) freshly squeezed lime juice
Cheesecloth

For the aguachile
9 ounces (250 g) frozen sea buckthorn berries (do not thaw)
1 ounce (28 g) frozen turmeric root, thawed
1 (3-ounce / 85-g) piece white saltwater fish, such as hake, cod, or flounder
Salt
Cheesecloth

For the cucumber salsa
1 pound (450 g) cucumbers, roughly chopped
1 cup (30 g) fresh cilantro

For serving
½ large red onion, cut into matchsticks
Juice of 1 lime, chilled
1 pound (450 g) Kampachi (or other sushi-grade tuna), sliced on the diagonal into 18 pieces
1 cucumber, cut into matchsticks (use any scraps for the salsa)
Nasturtium leaves

For the fish fumet base
In a high-powered blender, combine the ginger, red onion, garlic, lemongrass, celery, and habañeros with the lime juice and purée until smooth. Cover and refrigerate for about 1 hour, then strain through a fine-mesh strainer lined with cheesecloth.

For the aguachile
Fill a large bowl with ice water and set a smaller bowl inside.
Using a high-powered blender, purée the sea buckthorn berries and the turmeric with 1¾ cups (420 ml) of the fish fumet base until smooth. Add the white saltwater fish and 2¼ teaspoons of the salt then season to taste with more salt as needed. Strain through a fine-mesh sieve lined with cheesecloth into the bowl set in the ice bath. Keep cold.

For the cucumber salsa
In a high-powered blender, pulse the cucumbers and cilantro until roughly chopped together. Transfer to a strainer and allow the excess water to drain into a bowl or the sink.

For serving
In a small bowl, toss the red onion with the chilled lime juice. Pour about ½ cup (120 ml) of the aguachile into each of 6 chilled shallow bowls. Arrange 3 slices of kampachi in each bowl. Spoon some cucumber salsa alongside the fish then place the red onion and cucumber matchsticks on top. Cover with nasturtium leaves and serve immediately.

Daniela Soto-Innes

Striped Bass Moné with Mole Verde

Hoja santa, whose name means "sacred leaf," is prized in Mexico for its complex flavor, which is sometimes compared to licorice, anise, eucalyptus or even root beer. The velvety, heart-shaped leaves grow up to a foot across and can be found fresh in specialty Latin markets and some Southern farmers markets.

For the mole verde
2 cups (60 g) fresh cilantro leaves
⅓ ounce (10 g) fresh hoja santa leaves (pepper leaf)
1 cup (30 g) spinach
3 tablespoons grapeseed oil
2 tablespoons diced white onion
1 medium clove garlic, thinly sliced
½ fresh poblano pepper, seeded and julienned
2 ounces (60 g) fresh yellow chile, seeded and julienned
6 ounces (170 g) tomatillos, husked and cut into medium dice
¾ cup (180 ml) water
¼ pound (110 g) roasted pistachios
Salt

For the striped bass
6 (8-inch / 20-cm) banana leaf squares
6 fresh hoja santa leaves (pepper leaf), blanched and shocked
1 pound (450 g) striped bass fillets, cut into 6 equal portions
Extra-virgin olive oil, for drizzling
Freshly grated zest of 1 lemon
12 fresh epazote leaves
Salt

For serving
Extra-virgin olive oil, for drizzling
Fresh cilantro sprigs (or other herbs), for garnish

For the mole verde
Fill a large bowl with ice water and bring a large pot of salted water to a boil. Plunge the cilantro, hoja santa, and spinach into the boiling water and blanch for about 10 seconds or until bright green. Use tongs to transfer the leaves to the ice water. Squeeze excess water from the leaves and set aside.

In a medium saucepan, heat the grapeseed oil over medium heat. Add the onion and garlic and cook for about 2 minutes or until translucent. Add the poblano pepper and yellow chile and cook for 3 to 5 minutes or until soft. Add the tomatillos and cook for about 3 minutes or until starting to soften. Add the water and pistachios, bring to a simmer, and cook for about 5 minutes or until the tomatillos break down. Transfer to a blender or food processor and let cool to warm, then purée until smooth. Add the blanched cilantro, hoja santa, and spinach and blend until smooth. Season to taste with salt and transfer to a saucepan.

For the fish
Set up a steamer or put a round rack into a saucepan and add 1 to 2 inches (2.5 to 5 cm) of water.

Arrange a banana leaf square, shiny side down on a work surface then place an hoja santa leaf, shiny side down, on top. Set a piece of striped bass in the center of the hoja santa leaf, drizzle with a little extra-virgin olive oil, sprinkle with a little lemon zest, and top with 2 of the epazote leaves. Season to taste with salt then wrap the fish in the hoja santa leaf, followed by the banana leaf to form a bundle. Repeat with the remaining leaves and fish.

Bring the water in the steamer to a boil over high heat then reduce the heat to a simmer. Carefully set the fish bundles, folded-side down, in the steamer or on the rack, cover, and steam over medium heat for 8 minutes—the fish should be just cooked through.

For serving
Warm the mole verde over medium heat then ladle into 6 shallow bowls. Unwrap the fish bundles and transfer the hoja santa-wrapped fish to the bowls, discarding the banana leaves. Drizzle the fish with extra-virgin olive oil, garnish with cilantro or other herbs as desired, and serve hot.

New Zealand ⟶ Austin, Texas

Joseph Sukhendra

Born in New Zealand of Fiji Indian heritage, Joseph Sukhendra draws on his experience as a world traveler as he creates superior Southwest flavors in Austin, Texas.

During Sukhendra's childhood, cooking was central to his family and culture. He would often spend the whole day in the kitchen helping his grandmother cook breakfast, lunch and dinner. Inspired by her and by the two professional chefs in the family, Sukhendra was determined to perfect his craft and pursue a serious culinary career. He got his first restaurant job at age sixteen.

His first stop in the United States was Nashville, where he cooked under James Beard Award–nominated chef Tyler Brown at the Hermitage Hotel. Here, Sukhendra developed and refined his understanding of southern American cuisine and the revolutionary flavors of the New South.

Chef Andrew Wiseheart of Austin's award-winning Contigo recruited Sukhendra to join the team, which has earned awards from *Food & Wine* for several consecutive years. Sukhendra now oversees Contigo's extensive catering division, bringing superior cuisine to elite events. Guests savor dishes like fried quail leg, duck confit with carrot flower, and raspberry Pavlova with black pepper whipped cream.

"Being in an environment where there are different and diverse cultures has made me a better student, cook, and leader."

Joseph Sukhendra

Rosemary-Roasted Leg of Lamb and Mint Chutney

Serves 6 to 8

The classic pairing of lamb and mint gets a twist from green chutney spiked with ginger, garlic, and chile peppers.

For the lamb
6 to 8 cloves garlic, finely chopped
4 sprigs fresh rosemary, leaves finely chopped
2 to 3 tablespoons olive oil
1 heaping tablespoon salt
1 to 2 teaspoons freshly ground pepper
1 (4-pound / 1.8-kg) semi-boneless leg of lamb, trimmed

For the mint chutney
3 cups (150 g) finely chopped fresh mint
1 tablespoon finely chopped fresh ginger
1 tablespoon finely chopped garlic
1 tablespoon seeded and chopped fresh green chile, such as jalapeño or serrano
¼ cup (60 ml) extra-virgin olive oil
¼ cup (60 ml) freshly squeezed lemon juice
Salt

For the lamb
In a small bowl or food processor mix together the garlic, rosemary, olive oil, salt, and pepper until it looks like a paste. Using your hands, rub the paste all over the lamb, being sure to get into all the crevices. Place the lamb in a large bowl or container, cover, and refrigerate for 12 to 24 hours.

Preheat the oven to 325°F (160°C). Set the lamb in a roasting pan or on a large baking sheet and bake for 2 hours or until an instant-read thermometer inserted into the thickest part reads 125°F (52°C) for medium-rare. Let the lamb rest for 20 to 30 minutes. While the lamb rests, prepare the chutney.

For the mint chutney
In a medium bowl, mix together the mint, ginger, garlic, green chile, extra-virgin olive oil, and lemon juice. Season to taste with salt.

For serving
Carve the lamb and serve with the mint chutney.

Joseph Sukhendra

Banana Layer Cake with Vanilla Cream and Candied Walnuts

Makes 1 (8-inch / 20-cm) layer cake

This cake is made with two layers that are split in half horizontally, so there are four thin layers, each sandwiched with vanilla whipped cream. It's a naked cake, meaning the sides are left unfrosted. If you want to make this cake but don't have overripe bananas, bake unpeeled bananas at 300°F (150°F) until blackened and soft.

For the candied walnuts
½ pound (225 g) walnut pieces
½ cup (120 ml) honey
2 cups (200 g) confectioners' sugar

For the cake
1 cup plus 2 tablespoons (255 g)
    unsalted butter, softened
2 cups (400 grams) granulated
    sugar
4 large eggs
6 very ripe bananas, mashed
    (about 3 cups)
¼ cup (60 ml) whole milk, hot
2 teaspoons baking soda
4 cups (520 grams) all-purpose
    flour
2 teaspoons baking powder

For the vanilla cream
2 cups (480 ml) heavy whipping
    cream
¼ cup (25 g) confectioners' sugar
1 teaspoon vanilla extract
    (or vanilla bean paste)

For serving
Orange nasturtium leaves
    (optional)
Unopened lavender blossoms
    (optional)

For the candied walnuts
Preheat the oven to 350°F (180C).

Spread the walnuts on a baking sheet and bake for 3 to 5 minutes or until fragrant. Transfer the hot nuts to a large bowl, add the honey, and toss to coat. Transfer the walnuts to a fine strainer set over a bowl to drain off any excess honey.

Put the confectioners' sugar in a large shallow bowl. Add the drained nuts and toss until completely coated. Using a slotted spoon or a clean strainer with a handle, scoop up the nuts and tap off any excess sugar. Return the nuts to the baking sheet and bake for about 3 minutes or until just golden. Transfer to a cool baking sheet and let cool completely before using. Set aside some of the candied walnuts for serving. The rest will keep in an airtight container at room temperature for about 1 week.

For the cake
Preheat the oven to 350°F (180°C). Butter 2 (8-inch / 20-cm) round cake pans then dust with enough flour to completely cover the butter and tap out any excess.

In a large bowl, combine the butter and granulated sugar and use an electric mixer on medium-high speed to beat them together for about 4 minutes or until pale and fluffy. Add the eggs, 1 at a time, beating for 2 minutes after each addition. Mix in the mashed bananas. The batter will look broken, but this is ok.

In a small bowl, mix the hot milk with the baking soda then mix it into the batter.

In a large bowl, whisk together the flour and baking powder. Gradually fold the flour mixture into the batter until no streaks remain.

Transfer the batter to the prepared pans and bake for about 50 minutes or until the cakes spring back when lightly touched. Let the cakes rest for 20 minutes in the pans then turn them out onto a rack to cool completely. While the cakes bake and cool, prepare the vanilla cream.

For the vanilla cream
In a large bowl, use an electric mixer to whip the heavy whipping cream, confectioners' sugar, and vanilla until stiff peaks form. Cover and refrigerate for about 1 hour or until set.

For serving
Slice the top of each cooled cake layer to remove the dome shape and make the tops level then cut each layer in half horizontally so you have 4 even cake layers.

Arrange 1 cake layer, flat-side down, on a cake plate or other serving dish that will fit in the refrigerator. Using an offset spatula, spread about ¼ of vanilla cream on top, then arrange a second cake layer, flat-side up, on top. Repeat with the remaining vanilla cream and cake layers, finishing with a layer of vanilla cream, to create a 4-layer cake with naked sides. Refrigerate the cake for about 4 hours or until set.

Sprinkle the top of the cake with candied walnuts and, optionally, orange nasturtium leaves and unopened lavender blossoms, then slice and serve.

Kate Telfeyan

███████████████████

Kate Telfeyan was born in South Korea and abandoned in a supermarket as a baby. She arrived in the United States at the age of two, suffering from tuberculosis and severe malnutrition. Here she met her adoptive American family: a father of Armenian heritage, and a French-Canadian mother. She grew up enjoying the foods of both sides of the family but educated herself in Korean food, too. She spent a year studying in Spain and savoring Spanish flavors.

Telfeyan earned a degree in English literature and worked in publishing at Simon & Schuster, but longed for a culinary career. After a stint in public relations, helping Fatty Crab and other food businesses on menus and marketing, she joined a hospitality business, but the kitchen called her. She landed a cooking job at Ganso Ramen, climbed quickly, and went on to Mission Chinese Food, Chef Danny Bowien's groundbreaking Lower East Side hotspot serving creative riffs on Sichuan standards. She started cooking on the line there and quickly rose through the ranks. Today, she is the chef de cuisine.

"I was orphaned as a baby in South Korea; the authorities found me abandoned in a supermarket. When I arrived in the United States I was two years old, suffering from tuberculosis, and severely malnourished. My mother recounts my epic ability, as an infant, to eat four scrambled eggs in one sitting, and how I would hide bread under my leg for fear of food theft. I learned from an early age to not only desire food, but to understand my inherent need for the nourishment it provided, both physically and emotionally."

Kate Telfeyan

Sour Fish Soup

This fish soup has roots in my New England upbringing, but I season it with ingredients like Shaoxing wine, fermented fish sauce, and black vinegar to give it sour Chinese flavors.

For the fish
2 tablespoons Shaoxing wine (Chinese rice wine)
1 tablespoon cornstarch
1 pound (450 g) white fish, such as cod or hake, cut into 2 pieces

For the soup
2 tablespoons canola oil
½ cup (75 g) pepperoncini, minced, plus 1 cup (240 ml) pepperoncini liquid
2 tablespoons minced garlic
2 tablespoons finely grated fresh ginger
2 cups (480 ml) water
1 teaspoon mushroom powder
1 teaspoon fish sauce
½ teaspoon Chinese black vinegar
½ teaspoon granulated sugar
Salt and freshly ground white pepper
2 cups (110 g) rice flake noodles
Julienned red onion, roughly chopped cilantro stems, and chili oil, for garnish

For the fish
In a medium bowl, whisk together the Shaoxing wine and cornstarch until smooth. Add the fish and toss to coat. Let stand while you prepare the soup.

For the soup
In a wok or large saucepan, heat the canola oil until just glistening. Add the pepperoncini, garlic, and ginger, and cook, stirring frequently, for 3 to 4 minutes or until the pepperoncini are softened. Add the pepperoncini liquid and the water and bring to a boil. Add the mushroom powder, fish sauce, black vinegar, and sugar and season to taste with salt and white pepper. Continue boiling for 1 minute then add the fish and rice flake noodles and cook for 3 to 4 minutes or until the fish is cooked through and the noodles are softened. Garnish with the red onion and cilantro stems, drizzle with the chili oil to taste, and serve.

Kate Telfeyan

Hand-Torn Noodles with Cumin Lamb

Serves 2 to 4

Hand-torn noodles are a component of a traditional Korean dish called *sujebi*. I love to pair them with lamb, as an homage to my dad's Armenian heritage. Growing up, I was one of the only kids I knew who often had lamb for dinner. I finish this dish with flavors reminiscent of the cuisines of northern China.

For the noodles
2 cups (260 g) all-purpose flour
Salt
1 tablespoon vegetable oil
¾ cup (180 ml) water

For the herb salad
1 English cucumber, cut into
    matchsticks
1 bunch fresh dill, fronds picked
Juice of 1 lemon
Salt

For the lamb
2 tablespoons vegetable oil
½ white onion, diced
2 tablespoons minced shallot
1½ tablespoons minced garlic
3 tablespoons ground cumin
Ground cardamom
1 pound (450 g) ground lamb
3 tablespoons Chinese black
    vinegar
1 teaspoon fish sauce
Salt and freshly ground pepper
1 small handful chopped fresh
    cilantro stems
1 cup (240 ml) sour cream, thinned
    with the juice of 1 lemon

For the noodles
In a food processor fitted with the dough blade, combine the flour, ½ teaspoon of salt, and the vegetable oil. With the motor on, pour in the water and process for 30 to 45 seconds or until the dough starts coming up the sides of the bowl and forms a ball. Cover and let stand at room temperature for 30 minutes.

While the dough is resting, fill a medium saucepan with water and bring to a boil then add a big pinch of salt. Holding the ball of dough in one hand, use the index finger, middle finger, and thumb of your other hand to pull and tear off pieces of dough and carefully drop them into the boiling water. Continue with the remaining dough and cook for 2 to 3 minutes or until the noodles float to the surface. Drain the noodles and set aside.

For the herb salad
In a medium bowl, toss the cucumber matchsticks and dill fronds with the lemon juice, season to taste with salt, and set aside.

For the lamb
In a wok or large skillet, heat the vegetable oil over medium-high heat. Add the onion, shallot, and garlic and cook, stirring, for about 2 minutes or until the aromatics soften. Add the cumin and a pinch of cardamom and continue cooking for about 3 minutes or until the onions are translucent. Add the ground lamb and cook, using a spoon or chopsticks to break up the meat, for 3 to 4 minutes or until the lamb is mostly cooked through. Add the black vinegar and fish sauce and season to taste with salt and pepper. When the lamb is completely cooked, remove from the heat and add the cilantro stems.

Pour the lamb over the cooked noodles and toss to combine. Transfer to bowls, drizzle with the sour cream, top with the herb salad, and serve.

Simone Tong

████████████████████

Simone Tong was born in Chengdu, the capital of China's Sichuan Province. She studied in Chengdu, Beijing, Macau, Hong Kong, Singapore, and Australia, then graduated from UNC Chapel Hill in 2006 with degrees in economics and psychology.

Called to a culinary career, Tong eventually enrolled in the Institute of Culinary Education in New York City, graduating with highest honors. She went on to cook in some of the city's finest kitchens, including 15 East, and under Wylie Dufresne at WD-50 and Alder.

In 2016, she embarked on a three-month culinary and research adventure through Yunnan province. Starting from the capital city of Kunming, she visited the ancient towns of Dali and Lijiang, hiked through the Jade Dragon Snow Mountain and trekked through the breathtaking Tiger Leaping Gorge into the majestic Ganden Sumtseling Monastery in Shangri-La, bordering Tibet and Sichuan. She says that at each turn, she found a different magical recipe to learn and adapt. Now, as chef-owner of Little Tong Noodle Shop, Tong shares the story of the experience and the flavors and dishes experienced on her voyage. *New York Times* reviewer Pete Wells raved that he finished a bowl of her soup "in an astonished haze, and didn't regret it."

"Being an immigrant and a woman is a double whammy of challenges in the restaurant world. The chefs and teams I had mentored me through it all. They came from all walks of life, and their experiences and backgrounds challenged and shaped me. They were the fuel on which I was able to build two restaurants.

America was built by immigrants and now thrives because of them. We only become better when we come together not in spite of our differences, but because of them. That's the backbone on which my restaurant's largely female and immigrant team is structured, and it's the philosophy with which I approach my menu development, nurturing my team, and cultivating my guests' experience."

Simone Tong

Lala Wings

A chef once told me that Chinese cuisine is based on the principle 一方水土养一方人, meaning "each square of earth and water nurtures the people in that square." My restaurant focuses on *mixian*, which are rice noodles native to Yunnan, but the concept is that of a modern Chinese neighborhood restaurant centered around seasonality, locality, and techniques that pay respect to regional products, while paying homage to Yunnan's spirit and flavors. We don't follow a rigid definition of an "authentic" Yunnan restaurant, but we are authentic to the backgrounds and experiences of our team. The cuisine is created by and for the people of New York, who come from all walks of life, as well as the people of this great nation.

Fermented bean curd is optional, but you should be able to find it at Asian markets or online.

For the wings
1 small head garlic, chopped
1 tablespoon chopped fresh ginger
1 tablespoon chopped scallions
2 teaspoons Shaoxing wine (Chinese rice wine)
2 tablespoons plus 1 teaspoon tamari
1 tablespoon honey
Fish sauce
1 pound (450 g) chicken wings
Canola oil

For the wing sauce
¼ cup (60 ml) Sriracha sauce
1 tablespoon honey
½ ounce (15 g) fermented bean curd (optional)

For serving
1 tablespoon canola oil
1 teaspoon minced garlic
Lime slices
Chopped cilantro

For the wings
In a large bowl, whisk together the garlic, ginger, scallions, Shaoxing wine, tamari, honey, and a dash of fish sauce. Add the wings, toss to coat, cover, and refrigerate for 4 hours or overnight.

Preheat the oven to 325°F (160°C).

Rinse the marinade off the chicken wings then pat them dry with paper towels. Spread the wings in a single layer on a baking sheet, drizzle with canola oil, and toss to coat. Arrange the wings so they're skin-side up and bake for 10 minutes. Rotate the pan and bake for another 10 minutes. Raise the oven temperature to 400°F (200°C) and bake for 7 to 10 minutes or until fully cooked. While the wings are baking, make the wing sauce.

For the wing sauce
In a mini food processor, combine the Sriracha sauce, honey, and fermented bean curd, if using, plus a dash of water and purée until smooth.

For serving
In a large skillet, heat the canola oil over medium-high heat. Add the garlic and ¼ cup (60 ml) of the wing sauce and cook until sizzling. Add the baked wings and stir until fully coated with the sauce. Serve hot with lime slices, chopped cilantro, and additional wing sauce.

Simone Tong

Shrimp and Sausage Stir-Fry

Serves 4

Cooking under Wylie Dufresne, I learned to create and innovate, and to challenge the norm, while also respecting the culinary history and traditions that came before us. I want my food to be a means by which Americans can understand, appreciate, and ultimately live the togetherness and shared spirit of Chinese culture. I want to redefine and rethink authenticity in America.

1 cup plus 2 tablespoons (270 ml) water, cold
Salt
¼ pound (110 g) medium (41/50 count) or large (31/35 count) shrimp, peeled and deveined
1 tablespoon canola oil
4 links Chinese sausage, thinly sliced on a diagonal
1 teaspoon minced garlic
1 tablespoon Shaoxing wine (Chinese rice wine)
12 shishito peppers, cut on a diagonal into 3 pieces

In a large bowl, whisk together the cold water and 2½ teaspoons of salt.

Cut the shrimp so they're about the same size as the sausage pieces then add to the salt water and soak for 10 minutes. Drain the shrimp.

In a large skillet, heat the canola oil over medium heat. Add the Chinese sausage and cook, stirring, for about 1 minute or until the fat has been lightly rendered. Add the shrimp and cook for 1 minute, then add the garlic and stir to incorporate. Add the Shaoxing wine and cook, scraping up any browned bits from the bottom of the skillet. Add the shishito peppers and cook, stirring, for about 2 minutes or until the peppers are crisp-tender and the shrimp is fully cooked. Season to taste with salt and serve.

"From a young age I always dreamed of America. At seventeen, I wanted to go, experience, live my dream. In Serbia, I had experienced nothing but hardship. I knew things would not be good for me, no opportunities. People were struggling, unable to prosper. The only chance I would have for obtaining my goals and my potential would be in America. I knew that to achieve my dreams and be who I am today, I would only be able to do that here. That's what America is—since the creation of this country. Continuously."

Serbia ⟶ New York, New York

Miroslav Uskokovic

Miroslav Uskokovic's path to make prize-winning pastries in such vaunted New York restaurants as Wallsé, Jean-Georges, and Gramercy Tavern all began on his family's farm in Serbia. To survive the civil wars across the former Yugoslavia in the 1990s, Uskokovic's family grew their own food. His mother expertly produced the family's tart yogurt and cheese, and was beloved for her lofty breads and tender cakes. His father fed the family's chickens a seasonal diet of fruits and grains, producing eggs that still set the standard Uskokovic keeps for his rich custards and puffy Salzburger nockerls.

As a high school student, Uskokovic went on an exchange to Indiana and eventually applied to the Culinary Institute of America. While completing his externship at Wallsé, he had the chance to train at Jean-Georges, where he became pastry sous chef, and then went on to become the pastry chef at Aldea. Widely regarded as one of the top pastry chefs in North America, Uskokovic has developed a dessert menu at Gramercy Tavern featuring seasonal ingredients with a restrained European interpretation, including his show-stopping chocolate cake, a sweet homage to his late mother.

Miroslav Uskokovic

Ham and Cheese Piroške

Makes 10 to 12 piroške

Piroške are baked or fried stuffed buns. Originating in Russia, this delicious snack found its way to most of eastern and central Europe. In the western Balkans, including Serbia, piroške are usually shaped like logs and stuffed with cheese, ground meat, or sometimes both. My mother would often make them for breakfast or dinner. According to most Balkan moms, piroške are not considered appropriate for lunch, the most elaborate and ceremonious meal of the day, because they are almost embarrassingly easy to make!

For the dough
4½ cups (585 g) all-purpose flour
1½ pounds (680 g) feta, crumbled
4 large eggs
2 tablespoons olive oil
2 tablespoons granulated sugar
5 teaspoons baking powder

For the filling
10 to 12 slices ham (or prosciutto)
10 to 12 sticks mozzarella string
 cheese

For serving
Canola oil
Good-quality ketchup and pickles

For the dough
In a food processor, combine the flour, feta, eggs, olive oil, sugar, and baking powder and blend until a smooth and soft dough forms. Transfer the dough to a well-floured surface and knead briefly until it comes together in a ball. Place the ball of dough in an oiled bowl, cover with an inverted plate, and refrigerate for 4 to 24 hours.

For the filling
Wrap the ham around the mozzarella sticks and set aside.

Remove the dough from the refrigerator. On a floured work surface, use a rolling pin to roll out the dough to a large rectangle, about ¼ inch (0.5 cm) thick. Cut into 10 to 12 (4 x 6-inch / 10 x 15-cm) rectangles. Arrange a ham-wrapped mozzarella stick on the longer side of each rectangle then roll them up, sealing the edges well with a little bit of water. Roll gently on the floured work surface to shape into logs—they should look something like corn dogs.

Transfer the filled dough logs to a baking sheet or plate, cover with a kitchen towel, and chill for 1 to 4 hours. At this point you could also freeze the piroške for future use—freeze them in a single layer, then transfer to a resealable bag.

For serving
In a large, heavy-bottomed pot, heat 4 to 5 inches (10 to 12.5 cm) of canola oil to 325°F (160°C). Working in batches, gently add a couple piroške to the hot oil and fry, turning with a spoon to prevent cracks and ensure even browning, for 5 to 6 minutes or until the dough is cooked through and golden brown—some surface cracks may appear. If the dough is cooked, but the cheese is not melted, pop the piroške in a 325°F (160°F) oven for few minutes. Repeat to fry the remaining piroške and serve hot with ketchup and pickles.

Miroslav Uskokovic

Pancake Stack Cake

Makes 1 (9-inch / 23-cm) cake

This cake is Hungarian in origin, but it's also popular in parts of northern Serbia that were under Austro-Hungarian rule until the turn of the twentieth century. It's commonly called *Madjarska Palacinka Torta* or Hungarian Pancake Torte. Our mothers and grandmothers would typically bake it for Sunday lunch because it's so quick to make. The layers are somewhere between a pancake and a crêpe, and are sandwiched with various fillings. Almost always, there are walnuts, the most popular nut in the western Balkans. As my aunt used to say: "It isn't a cake if it doesn't have walnuts."

For the raspberry jam
18 ounces (500 g) raspberries
2½ cups (500 g) granulated sugar
2 tablespoons freshly squeezed
lemon juice

For the filling
3 ounces (85 g) walnuts, toasted
and cold
3 ounces (85 g) bittersweet
chocolate, chopped and cold

For the cake
6 large eggs, separated
1¼ cups (135 g) confectioners'
sugar
Salt
1⅓ cups (175 g) cake flour
1 cup (130 g) all-purpose flour
1 tablespoon maple syrup
⅓ cup (75 ml) canola oil
1⅔ cups (390 ml) whole milk
¾ cup plus 1 tablespoon (195 ml)
half-and-half
Unsalted butter, melted

For serving
1 pint (250 g) raspberries
Edible flowers (optional)
Confectioners' sugar

For the raspberry jam
Place a small plate in the freezer.

In a medium, heavy-bottomed pan, combine half of the raspberries with the sugar over high heat and bring to a boil, stirring often. Continue boiling, while stirring and gradually lowering the heat, as the jam starts to thicken. After about 1 5 minutes, add the remaining raspberries. Mix well and cook, stirring constantly, for another 10 to 15 minutes or until the jam is ready.

To test the jam, spoon a small dollop onto the frozen plate. It should hold its shape and wrinkle lightly when you run your finger through it.

Remove the pan from the heat and let the jam cool to warm. Stir in the lemon juice and use an immersion blender to slightly purée the jam. Spoon the raspberry jam into a piping bag and set aside.

For the filling
In a food processor, pulse the cold walnuts and chocolate together until finely ground. Be careful not to over-process as this may melt the chocolate or release the oils in the walnuts. Refrigerate until ready to use.

For the cake
Using an electric mixer or a stand mixer fitted with the whisk attachment, whip the egg whites, about half of the confectioners' sugar, and a generous pinch of salt at medium speed until a meringue with soft peaks forms.

Sift the cake and all-purpose flours together into a medium bowl.

In a clean bowl, use the mixer to whip the egg yolks with the remaining confectioners' sugar until they triple in volume. Add the maple syrup, followed by the canola oil, and mix until combined. With the mixer running, add the milk, followed by the half-and-half, in a slow steady stream. Add the flour mixture and mix until the batter is smooth with no visible lumps.

Continued $\longrightarrow$

Miroslav Uskokovic

Using a whisk, gently fold the meringue into the batter in 3 additions then switch to a spatula to reach the sides and bottom of the bowl. Make sure the meringue is well incorporated with no chunks of egg white.

Arrange a platter or cake stand, the walnut-chocolate mixture, and the piping bag filled with jam next to the stove, so you can assemble the cake as you work.

Heat a 9-inch (23 cm) nonstick skillet over medium heat. Brush the skillet lightly with melted butter and pour in about ½ cup (120 ml) of the batter. It should spread on its own and cover the bottom of the skillet. Cook, without flipping, until the bottom of the crêpe is lightly browned and bubbles appear on top—the top will look creamy and just set. Carefully shimmy the crêpe out of the skillet and onto your platter or cake stand then sprinkle generously with some of the walnut-chocolate mixture and evenly pipe about ⅓ cup (75 ml) of jam on top. Continue to cook crêpes and layer with the walnut-chocolate mixture and jam— you should be able to make about 9 crêpes. For the very last layer, flip the crêpe so the browned side that was in contact with the skillet is on top and do not add the walnut-chocolate mixture or jam.

For serving
Scatter the raspberries and edible flowers, if using, on top of the cake, dust with confectioners' sugar, and serve warm.

Philippines $\longrightarrow$ New York, New York

Harold Villarosa

███████████████████████████████

Harold Villarosa received his earliest food education in rice paddies in his native Philippines. His family immigrated to New York, where he was raised in the hardscrabble Bronx and found work in a McDonald's. He would soon move on to some of the greatest restaurants in the world.

At Macondo and Rayuela restaurants, he found an early mentor, the late chef Máximo Tejada. Working hard and showing serious talent, Villarosa found himself with an invitation from Chef René Redzepi to cook at the top rated restaurant in the world, Noma in Copenhagen. Back in New York, he staged at Michelin-starred restaurants like Aquavit, Aureole, and Rouge Tomate. Gleaning kitchen skills from places like Fedora in the West Village and learning restaurant operations at Batard—the 2015 recipient of the James Beard Award for Best Restaurant—Villarosa worked his way up the culinary ladder to chef Thomas Keller's ground-breaking four-star restaurant, Per Se.

Villarosa is now head chef at Well& in New York City. He holds a culinary arts degree from the Culinary Academy of New York and is a member of the Black Culinary Alliance and the Experimental Cuisine Collective in conjunction with New York University's Chemistry Department.

Villarosa's community collective, Insurgo (Latin for "to go against the grain"), is focused on farm-to-table movements in low-income neighborhoods. As a man raised in what we now call a "food desert," and whose first job was in the fast food industry, he strives to provide young people with opportunities in the international culinary movement. Villarosa and Insurgo organize community tastings, elementary and high school curriculum development, free educational panels, and fundraising events.

"I felt so much pride adapting myself into my new home. Learning to quickly adapt really helped me maneuver well in the culinary industry. I was this brown kid, burns all up his arms, very eager to learn, getting into the kitchen by sheer will and hard work. My kitchen now is all immigrants, people who are willing to work as hard as possible to see a better life for their families and for themselves. It's fulfilling work and I'm proud to say I'm an immigrant in this country who has pushed it."

Harold Villarosa

Salmon Belly with Sweet-and-Sour Glaze, Miso-Mushroom Purée, and Herb Salad

Serves 4

My cooking style is farm-to-table and nose-to-tail—in this case, that's fish tail. I always try to use the whole animal, without any waste.

For the miso-mushroom purée
2 tablespoons canola oil
2 pounds (900 g) button
  mushrooms, thinly sliced
2 cloves garlic, smashed
1 shallot, diced
2 sprigs fresh thyme
¼ cup (60) white wine
2 cups (480 ml) whole milk
2 cups (480 ml) heavy cream
3 tablespoons white miso
1 cup (225 g) unsalted butter,
  diced and cold
Salt and freshly ground pepper

For the sweet-and-sour glaze
1 cup (240 ml) pineapple juice
½ cup (120 ml) rice vinegar
¼ cup (60 ml) ketchup
½ cup (100 g) light brown sugar
1 teaspoon salt
1 tablespoon cornstarch
1 tablespoon canola oil
½ small green bell pepper,
  seeded and minced

For serving
2 pieces skin-on salmon belly,
  7 ounces to ¾ pound
  (200 to 340 g) each
1 bunch fresh cilantro leaves and
  tender stems
1 bunch fresh mint
1 bunch fresh Thai basil
1 bunch fresh chives, cut into 3 to
  4-inch (7.5 to 10 cm) pieces

For the miso-mushroom purée
In a large saucepan, heat the canola oil over medium heat. Add the mushrooms, garlic, shallot, and thyme and cook for 5 to 7 minutes or until the mushrooms are softened. Add the white wine and cook for about 1 minute or until evaporated. Add the milk, heavy cream, and miso then reduce the heat to low and cook for about 25 minutes or until the liquid is infused with the flavor.

Strain the liquid into a large measuring cup. Remove and discard the thyme then transfer the solids to a food processor or blender. Add just enough of the liquid to get the purée going and start blending on high speed. With the machine on, add the cubes of butter and more of the liquid until the purée reaches a consistency you like. Season to taste with salt and pepper. For a smooth purée, push it through a very fine strainer.

For the sweet-and-sour glaze
In a medium bowl, whisk together the pineapple juice, rice vinegar, ketchup, light brown sugar, and salt until the sugar and salt are dissolved. Add the cornstarch and whisk until fully incorporated.

In a small saucepan, heat the canola oil over medium heat. Add the bell pepper and cook, stirring frequently, until softened. Add the pineapple juice mixture and bring to a boil, whisking frequently. Continue boiling and whisking frequently for 2 to 3 minutes or until the glaze thickens. Keep warm.

For serving
Set the oven to broil. Arrange the salmon belly pieces, skin-side down, on a baking sheet and broil about 4 inches (10 cm) from the heat for about 4 minutes or until starting to brown on top. Flip the fish and broil for about 5 minutes or until the skin is charred. (Alternatively, grill the salmon belly, skin-side down and without flipping, over medium-high heat for 8 to 10 minutes.)

Pull the cilantro, mint, and Thai basil into separate leaves and sprigs. In a bowl, toss them together with the chives.

Arrange the salmon belly, skin-side up, on 2 platters and brush with the glaze. Spoon some of the mushroom purée alongside. Top each platter with the herb salad and drizzle with more of the glaze if desired. Serve hot.

Curry-Braised Lamb Belly

Serves 4

This recipe calls for 5 pounds (2.3 kg) of lamb belly for four people, but don't worry—a lot of fat gets trimmed off. If you can find pre-trimmed lamb belly, use just 2 to 3 pounds (900 g to 1.4 kg). Render any leftover fat and save it for cooking potatoes.

For the curry paste
4 cloves garlic, roughly chopped
3 ounces (85 g) shallots, roughly chopped
2 ounces (60 g) fresh ginger, roughly chopped
1 ounce (28 g) fresh turmeric, roughly chopped
¾ ounce (20 g) fresh or frozen makrut lime leaves
½ ounce (15 g) fresh red Thai chiles, roughly chopped

For the lamb belly
5 pounds (2.3 kg) lamb belly, trimmed of excess fat and cut into 2-inch (5 cm) chunks
Salt and freshly ground pepper
2 tablespoons canola oil
3 onions, diced
2 large carrots, diced
1 pound (450 g) new potatoes
10 cloves garlic, thinly sliced
1 (14-ounce / 414 ml) can coconut milk, preferably Vietnamese
4 cups (960 ml) water
Steamed white rice, for serving
Roasted and salted peanuts, chopped, for garnish
Cilantro, for garnish (optional)
Fried shallots, for garnish (optional)
Edible flowers, for garnish (optional)

For the curry paste
In a food processor, combine the garlic, shallots, ginger, turmeric, makrut lime leaves, and Thai chiles and pulse until finely chopped then process until a paste forms.

For the lamb belly
Season the lamb belly with salt and pepper. In a large Dutch oven, heat the canola oil over medium-high heat until shimmering. Working in batches, add the lamb belly in a single layer and cook, turning as necessary, until browned all over.Repeat to brown all the lamb and transfer it to a plate, but leave the Dutch oven on the heat. Add the onions, carrots, potatoes, and garlic and cook, stirring occasionally, for about 4 minutes or until the onions are translucent. Add the curry paste and cook for about 3 minutes or until fragrant and starting to color. Add the coconut milk and water, return the lamb belly to the Dutch oven, and bring to a boil. Reduce the heat to medium-low and simmer for about 2 hours or until the lamb belly is fork-tender. Season to taste with salt and pepper. Spoon into bowls with steamed white rice, garnish with peanuts and, optionally, cilantro, fried shallots, and edible flowers, and serve.

Mexico ——→ New York, New York

Fabián von Hauske Valtierra

When Fabián von Hauske Valtierra was growing up in Mexico City, his father often took the family along on business trips around the world, complete with visits to some of the best restaurants on Earth. Young Fabián set his sights on a serious culinary career and, at age seventeen, moved to New York City to pursue that dream. After graduating from the French Culinary Institute (now the International Culinary Center), he cooked at some of the world's greatest restaurants, including Jean Georges in New York, Noma in Copenhagen, Faviken in Sweden, and Attica in Melbourne.

After returning to New York, just 23 years old, he and partner Jeremiah Stone opened Contra, a tasting menu-only restaurant on the Lower East Side, and were awarded a Michelin star. Their second and third restaurants, Wildair and Una Pizza Napoletana, have also earned rave national reviews.

Though Contra was an instant success, von Hauske Valtierra faced hurdles renewing his visa. Finally, in 2016, he was granted permanent residency. "Getting a green card based on my merits is perhaps the greatest reward I've gotten in my time as a chef in this country," he says.

Von Hauske Valtierra now strives to mentor and empower his employees. A third of his kitchen staff are immigrants. "Hopefully, they can then pay it forward, and the change keeps going and going."

He says that his winning the Vilcek Prize for Creative Promise is a validation for all immigrants in the US, especially now, when many feel pressure to give up on their dreams and move home. Von Hauske Valtierra urges them to keep striving. "Being an immigrant here," he says, "you can create change."

"Things that are natural for all humans—music, food, art—those are the best ways to connect and create bonds across cultures. So I've always thought the only way a culture and society will go forward is through the acceptance of different cultures. I feel very strongly that if I meet someone who is not from here, but has the ability to do something great, then I should be the one who empowers them, because I've been through it, and I take a lot of pride and pleasure in helping those people out. The more foreigners you have, they'll make this place their home, and better this place. That's how I feel."

Fabián von Hauske Valtierra

Little Gem Lettuce with Pistachio and Herbs

Serves 4

Lots of people think the pistachio cream here is avocado, which would make this the avocado toast of salads, but it's not. The best part of this dish is that the leaves here are intact, so they don't get dressed in a conventional way—kind of a more elegant wedge salad. The nuts and herbs get incorporated as you eat, making it more of an interactive experience, mixing and seasoning as you go.

4 heads Little Gem lettuce, halved lengthwise
½ cup plus 6 tablespoons (210 g) unsalted butter
Salt
1 large egg yolk
¼ pound (110 g) raw pistachios, chopped
Freshly squeezed lemon juice
Extra-virgin olive oil
Freshly ground pepper
1½ ounces (45 g) fresh chives, chopped
1½ ounces (45 g) fresh chervil leaves

Remove the outer leaves of the little gems until you have 8 perfect little halves and set them aside; reserve the leaves you removed.

In a large skillet, melt the butter over medium heat. Add the reserved lettuce leaves, season to taste with salt, and cook, stirring, for about 1 minute or until wilted. Transfer the leaves and butter to a blender. Add the egg yolk and a little less than half of the pistachios and blend until smooth and creamy. The mixture should have the consistency of yellow mustard. If it's too thin, add more pistachios, and if it's too thick, add a little water. Season to taste with salt.

Use a knife to crush the remaining pistachios.

Dress the little gem halves to taste with lemon juice, extra-virgin olive oil, salt, and pepper. Drizzle the pistachio cream over the top and scatter with the chives, chervil, and crushed pistachios.

Fabián von Hauske Valtierra

Panna Cotta with Cantaloupe Granita

Serves 4

At Wildair, the desserts are meant to be simple and familiar and honestly it doesn't get much simpler or more familiar than panna cotta. Our recipe is different from most others because we only cook a small amount of cream just to melt the gelatin, but leave the majority uncooked. Cooking dairy changes the flavor completely and I just prefer the freshness of uncooked cream.

Panna cotta goes with every fruit, so we change the granita with the seasons. Concord grape is my favorite, but cantaloupe is a close second.

For the salted caramel sauce
1 cup (200 g) granulated sugar
1½ teaspoons glucose
¼ cup plus 3 tablespoons (105 ml) heavy cream, at room temperature
¼ cup (60 g) unsalted butter
1 teaspoon salt

For the milk crumble
⅓ cup (45 g) all-purpose flour
⅓ cup (38 g) milk powder
¼ cup (60 g) unsalted butter
3 tablespoons plus 2 teaspoons granulated sugar
Salt

For the cantaloupe granita
1½ pounds (680 g) cantaloupe, peeled and seeded
3 tablespoons granulated sugar, plus more to taste
1 tablespoon plus 1 teaspoon freshly squeezed lemon juice, plus more to taste
Salt

For the panna cotta
1½ sheets silver-grade gelatin
2 cups (480 ml g) heavy cream
1 tablespoon plus 1 teaspoon granulated sugar
1 teaspoon salt
½ vanilla bean

For the salted caramel sauce
In a medium saucepan, combine the sugar, glucose, and just enough cold water to create a wet sand texture. Bring to a simmer over medium-high heat and continue simmering until the mixture reaches 340°F (170°C) and is a dark amber color. Check the color by using a whisk to drizzle the caramel on a white plate. (Do not judge the color by how the caramel looks in the pot, because by the time it looks dark enough in the pot, it will be too dark.) Slowly and carefully whisk in the heavy cream—it will sputter—followed by the butter and salt and continue whisking until everything is well emulsified and incorporated. Let cool completely.

For the milk crumble
Preheat the oven to 325°F (160°C). Line a baking sheet with a silicone liner or parchment paper.

In a food processor, combine the flour, milk powder, butter, sugar, and a pinch of salt and process until sandy. Spread onto the parchment-lined baking sheet and bake, tossing every 5 minutes or so, for 8 to 12 minutes or until golden brown.

Continued ⟶

Fabián von Hauske Valtierra

For the cantaloupe granita

Using a juicer, juice the cantaloupe. (Alternatively, process the canta-loupe in a blender and then strain it.) Add the sugar, lemon juice, and a pinch of salt. Season to taste with more sugar or lemon juice. Pour into a freezer-safe 9 x 13-inch (23 x 33 cm) baking dish and freeze for 10 to 12 hours or until completely firm. Using a large fork, scrape the granita until it's super fluffy and fine. Keep frozen until ready to use.

For the panna cotta

Fill a large bowl with ice water and soak the gelatin until completely soft.

In a medium saucepan, combine ½ cup (120 ml) of the heavy cream with the sugar and salt. Split the vanilla bean and scrape out the seeds then add the bean and seeds to the heavy cream mixture and bring to a simmer over medium heat. Squeeze the water from the gelatin, reserving the ice water, then add the gelatin to the heavy cream mixture and stir to dissolve. Remove the pot from the heat and set in the ice bath to cool completely. Stir in the remain-ing 1½ cups (360 ml) heavy cream.

Remove the vanilla bean then divide the heavy cream mixture among 4 shallow bowls, cover, and refrigerate to set for 8 to 10 hours or preferably overnight.

For serving

Unmold the panna cotta if desired or leave them in the bowls. Drizzle with the salted caramel sauce and milk crumble, if using, top with the granita, and serve.

China ⟶ Charleston, South Carolina

Shuai Wang

███████████████

Shuai Wang is the chef and co-owner of Short Grain, an untraditional Japanese pop-up restaurant that focuses on heritage-driven, local, sustainable fare in Charleston, South Carolina. Born in Beijing, Wang was educated at the Art Institute of New York and rose through the ranks in Manhattan kitchens, including a stint as sous chef at Joseph Leonard and a job as chef de cuisine at Chez Sardine. Moving to Charleston, however, inspired Wang's own creative vision.

Now he's one face of the Charleston culinary renaissance, offering a new take on Japanese food at Short Grain, which was named by *Bon Appétit* as one of the Top 50 Best New Restaurants of 2016. In the process, Wang began thoughtfully crossing Asian ingredients with flavors of the New South.

Focused on local produce and the freshest Low Country seafood, Short Grain serves creative culinary combinations: lump crab fried rice with ponzu, snapper stew with spicy kimchi, and shrimp with rice "grits" are all part of the constellation of food that the chef believes can bring people together across cultures.

In 2016, Wang won Eater's Young Gun award, made the Charleston *Zagat* 30 Under 30 list, and was named Eater's Best New Chef, Charleston. In 2017, he was nominated by the James Beard Foundation as a semi-finalist for the Rising Star award. His new restaurant Jackrabbit Filly, a celebration of his Chinese heritage, opened in Park Circle, South Carolina, in 2019.

"We're here to break barriers through delicious food. Lin-Manuel Miranda said that love is love is love is love; we like to say, food is food is food is food. America's a big melting pot, and there shouldn't be your food, my food, their food, but only our food."

Shuai Wang

Southern Veggie Poke

Americans have fallen in love with Hawaiian poke, an Asian-inflected dish featuring raw fish that's cut into chunks and marinated with soy sauce and scallions. This Southern vegetarian version features beets, corn, tomatoes, and that Deep South garden favorite: butter beans. Furikake is available at Japanese markets or online.

½ cup (120 ml) Kewpie mayonnaise
1 tablespoon soy sauce
1 tablespoon freshly grated lemon zest
1 tablespoon freshly squeezed lemon juice
2 teaspoons Sriracha sauce
2 teaspoons honey
1 teaspoon toasted sesame oil
1 clove garlic, minced
½ teaspoon freshly ground pepper
1 pint (250 g) cherry tomatoes, quartered
1½ cups (225 g) cooked butter beans
1 cup (200 g) peeled and chopped cooked beets
1 cup (140 g) cooked yellow corn kernels
2¼ cup (150 g) cooked sushi rice
2 tablespoons furikake, preferably nori komi
3 cups (60 g) loosely packed fresh arugula

In a medium bowl, whisk together the mayonnaise, soy sauce, lemon zest and juice, the Sriracha sauce, honey, toasted sesame oil, garlic, and pepper. The dressing can be made ahead and refrigerated for up to 24 hours.

In a large bowl, toss together the cherry tomatoes, butter beans, beets, and corn. Add ¼ cup (60 ml) of the dressing and stir until well combined.

Divide the sushi rice evenly among 4 bowls, top each with the vegetable mixture, and sprinkle with the furikake. Top each bowl with arugula, drizzle with more dressing to taste, and serve with additional dressing alongside.

Shuai Wang

Coconut Beef Curry

This curry relies on just a few supermarket ingredients to create big flavor. For that reason, use the best quality curry powder you can find, or at least, open a fresh jar. It will be worth it.

1½ pounds beef chuck (680 g), cut into 1½-inch (4 cm) pieces
Kosher salt
2 tablespoons vegetable oil
2 tablespoons unsalted butter
½ large white onion, thinly sliced
4 garlic cloves, finely chopped
1 tablespoon finely chopped fresh ginger
3 tablespoons curry powder
2 bay leaves
2 (14-ounce / 414 ml) cans coconut milk
1 cup (240 ml) water, plus more as needed
2 pounds (900 g) Yukon gold potatoes, peeled and cut into 2-inch (5 cm) pieces
Steamed jasmine rice, Thai basil leaves, thinly sliced Fresno chile, and lime wedges, for serving

Season the beef generously with salt. In a large, heavy pot or Dutch oven, heat the oil over medium-high. Working in batches as needed, add the beef and cook, turning occasionally, until deeply browned all over, 8 to 10 minutes. Transfer to a plate.

Pour off all but 1 tablespoon of fat from the pot and reduce the heat to medium. Add the butter, onion, garlic, and ginger, and cook, stirring often and scraping up the browned bits from the bottom of the pot, until the onion is translucent, about 5 minutes. Add the curry powder, and cook, stirring, until it starts to stick to the bottom of the pot, about 3 minutes. Stir in the bay leaves, coconut milk, and water. Return the beef to the pot, season with salt, and bring to a simmer. Cook, partially covered, until the beef is just barely fork-tender, 30 to 35 minutes.

Add the potatoes; bring to a simmer, and cook uncovered, stirring occasionally, until the beef and potatoes are very tender, 40 to 50 minutes longer. Check the consistency of the liquid, and if it seems too thick, add a little more water to thin. Season the curry with salt, then serve over rice with Thai basil, chile, and lime wedges.

Nigeria ⟶ New Orleans, Louisiana

Tunde Wey

Tunde Wey is a chef and writer working at the intersection of food and social politics. His food may be delicious but his goal is also discomfort.

Born in Lagos, Nigeria, Wey arrived in the US on a student visa but received an additional education in being black in the US as an undocumented immigrant. Despite success as a co-owner in a concept restaurant in Detroit, Wey found the constraints of New American cuisine too superficial for the conversations on race, gentrification, and displacement he felt were urgent in his community. Returning to the flavors in Nigerian cuisine, Wey has designed his dinner pop-ups to introduce Americans to the West African palate anchored by cassava, eggplant, palm oil, and yams as well as powerful social concepts.

Today his work uses food to understand race, power, imperialism, wealth disparity, and access. In his cross-country dinner series and his pop-up meals, Wey offers his analysis using examples as diverse as Jay-Z and a South African woman exploited as the "Venus Hottentot" exhibit in nineteenth-century Europe.

His lunch counter concept, Saartjie, offered Nigerian plate lunches and a provocative price structure: white customers were invited to pay two and half times the price charged to black patrons, as a form of reparations.

Wey's food work has been featured in the *New York Times, Washington Post*, and on NPR. His own writing has been published in the *Boston Globe, Oxford American* and CityLab. He writes a column in the *San Francisco Chronicle*.

"My immigrant identity and the experience of marginalization—manifest in all spaces because I am marked by a foreign name, an accent, and a troubled skin color—impelled my cooking to interrogate not just the Euro-centricity and whiteness of food culture but larger systems of exploitative power. I cook Nigerian food now as oppositional food, situating it in the tradition of other resistance movements in the arts and civic space that offered counter narratives and positions to dominant and oppressive systems."

Tunde Wey

Steamed Plantain Cakes (Ukpo Ogede)

Ukpo ogede is a southwestern Nigerian delicacy. Similar to *moi moi* (steamed bean cakes), ukpo ogede is made with overly ripe plantains, which give the dish a characteristic sweet flavor that's balanced by the savory umami of the other ingredients. These are a little like tamales, and often served with Nigerian custard. Traditionally, large fan-like green leaves called *uma* are used to wrap the batter for steaming, but corn husks work well, too. Look for *iru*, fermented locust bean, at African markets.

3 soft black plantains, peeled and coarsely chopped
½ onion, coarsely chopped
1 red bell pepper, seeded and coarsely chopped
½ fresh habañero chile, seeded (optional) and coarsely chopped
½ cup (120 ml) water
Salt
Powdered iru (fermented locust bean), for seasoning
10 dried corn husks
Fresh figs, for serving

In a food processor or blender, combine the plantains, onion, red bell pepper, habañero, and water and purée until smooth. Season to taste with salt and iru. Transfer to a bowl.

Arrange the dried corn husks on a work surface and scoop about about ¼ cup (60 g) of the batter onto each husk. Fold the husk over the batter crosswise and then lengthwise to form little bundles. Arrange the corn husk bundles with the folded sides down on a platter or baking sheet.

Set up a steamer pot or arrange a round rack in the bottom of a large pot. Fill the pot with a few inches of water, making sure the steaming rack is not submerged, and bring to a boil. Carefully set the corn husk bundles in the steamer then cover, lower the heat, and steam, adding more water as needed, for about 45 minutes or until a knife inserted in the center of the filling comes out clean. Serve immediately alongside fresh figs.

Nite Yun

"Cooking is a way of uncovering my history. My parents escaped Cambodia during the Khmer Rouge genocide. I was born in a refugee camp. When I moved to San Francisco, no one knew Cambodian food. To Americans, Cambodia simply meant violence and war. But Cambodia has a beautiful history and resilient people. I wanted to tell this story through a restaurant.

Now in the dining room, we have people from all backgrounds. This is why I started Nyum Bai. To celebrate Cambodia, through its beautiful food. I want to make other immigrants feel that they can accomplish anything. When I look back at where I'm from, it was hard to imagine being successful. There were so many challenges, a language barrier, seeing my parents struggle. But if you work hard enough anything is possible. Don't let the hardship define you. It will help you instead.

I want my restaurant, my food, my career to be an indication that you can find your own way, cook your own food, and create your own community."

Nite Yun's parents fled the Cambodian genocide in 1976. She was born in a refugee camp in Thailand and when she was two, the family came to the US as refugees. Space was tight in the one-bedroom California apartment where they lived. Her father was often away picking produce or clocking hours at a Chinese restaurant, so Yun would join her mother in the kitchen, chopping lemongrass, gutting fish, sharpening knives—and learning all the while.

Those skills and recipes now form the foundation of Yun's smash-hit Oakland restaurant, Nyum Bai, whose name is Cambodian for "Let's eat!", and the Bay Area lined up to take heed. The dining room is regularly crowded with a mix of Cambodians and non-Cambodians alike, all of whom come to feast on Yun's made-from-scratch curries, noodles, soups, fried chicken, and more. Within months of the restaurant's opening, Yun won national critical acclaim, including a spot on *Bon Appétit*'s 2018 Hot Ten list of Best New Restaurants in the US. She is also is one of the winners of the 2019 Vilcek Prize for Creative Promise in Culinary Arts, and a 2019 *Food & Wine* Best New Chef.

"Cambodian is a cuisine that's been lost," Yun says, "But now it's being revived again."

Nite Yun

Fried Fish Fillets with Mango Salad (Trei Jien)

Serves 2

I learned to cook in a small one-bedroom apartment, living with my parents and two brothers in California. My brothers would shoo me away and I had nowhere to go but the kitchen to help my mom with the daily cooking, making recipes like this. I smashed garlic, cut lemongrass, gutted fish, sharpened knives, and used a mortar and pestle to make spice pastes or extract milk from coconuts. Years later, I traveled to Cambodia to get the answers about my parents that they wouldn't give me. These recipes are my history.

For the mango salad
⅓ cup plus 1 tablespoon (90 ml) freshly squeezed lime juice
¼ cup (60 ml) fish sauce
2 tablespoons dark brown sugar
2½ teaspoons granulated sugar
2 teaspoons canola oil
Salt
1 green (firm, unripe) mango, peeled and julienned
2 scallions, thinly sliced
1 small shallot, preferably Asian, thinly sliced
2 teaspoons minced fresh bird's eye chile
¼ teaspoon minced garlic
1 cup (30 g) fresh Thai basil leaves

For the fish
1 cup (140 g) rice flour
1 teaspoon baking powder
Salt
½ cup (120 ml) water
2 firm fish fillets, such as catfish, about 7 ounces (200 g) each
Canola oil

For serving
Roasted and salted peanuts, crushed, for garnish
Steamed jasmine rice, for serving

For the mango salad
In a large bowl, whisk together the lime juice, fish sauce, dark brown sugar, granulated sugar, canola oil, and a pinch of salt. Just before serving, add the mango, scallions, shallot, bird's eye chile, garlic, and Thai basil and toss to combine.

For the fish
In a medium bowl, whisk together the rice flour, baking powder, and a pinch of salt. Add the water and stir to combine. The mixture should resemble pancake batter, so add a little more water as needed to get the right consistency.

Line a plate with paper towels and arrange near the stove. In a deep skillet or wok, heat about ½ inch (1.25 cm) of canola oil over medium heat until just shimmering. Season the fish fillets with salt then dip in the batter. Carefully add the battered fish to the hot oil and fry, turning once, for 2 to 3 minutes per side or until golden. Transfer to the prepared plate to drain.

For serving
Arrange the fish on plates, then top with the mango salad, garnish with crushed peanuts, and serve with rice.

Nite Yun

Coconut Milk–Marinated Pork with Rice (Bai Sach Chrouk)

Serves 2

My cooking is a way of uncovering my own history and roots, as well as offering a space for kids like me, who have often felt like they don't know where they belong. My restaurant, Nyum Bai, was born out of a search for my parents but also a search for myself. I found my recipes on trips back to Cambodia, but I know that my community is here in Oakland, and in other cities in America, where people like me are charting their own paths.

1 cup (240 ml) coconut milk
¼ cup (50 g) dark brown sugar
4 cloves garlic, minced
1 tablespoon fish sauce
2 teaspoons freshly ground pepper
½ pound (225 g) pork loin,
    thinly sliced
1 tablespoon canola oil
Steamed jasmine rice, fried eggs,
    pickled red onion, and salad,
    for serving

In a large bowl, whisk together the coconut milk, dark brown sugar, garlic, fish sauce, and pepper. Add the pork and turn to coat then cover and refrigerate for 4 to 24 hours.

Remove the pork from the marinade and transfer to a plate.

In a grill pan, heat the canola oil over medium-high heat until shimmering. Working in batches as needed, add the pork and cook, turning once, for 2 to 3 minutes or until browned all over. Repeat with the remaining pork and serve with jasmine rice, fried eggs, pickled red onion, and salad.

Index

A

Abdullahi, Fariyal, *8–13*
adobo, pork, *93*
aguachile, sea buckthorn, with cucumber and kampachi, *191*
Aikawa, Tatsu, *14–19*
aïoli, lovage, *75–77*
aji ammarillo paste, *59*
amaranth, *25–27*
anchovies with potato salad, *101*
Andrés, José, *55*
apples
    with gravlax, *23*
    pickled, with vanilla-cured duck breasts, *69*
apricots, dried, in coffee-braised brisket, *179*
Argentina, *116–21, 152–57*
arugula, in Southern veggie poke, *237*
asazuke pickles, *17, 19*
asparagus
    with spicy pork lettuce wraps, *105*
    and spring barley, *25–27*
Austin, Texas, *14–19, 194–99*
avocadoes, in ceviche nikkei, *57*

B

bacon, in takoyaki hush puppies, *31*
bai sach chrouk, *249*
bananas
    in bibingka, *133*
    layer cake with vanilla cream and candied walnuts, *199*
    in teff pancakes, *11*
barley and spring vegetables, *25–27*
Barrett, Donna, *173*
Bayless, Rick, *67*
beans, butter, in Southern veggie poke, *237*
beef
    brisket, coffee-braised, *179*
    coconut curry, *239*
    Helga's meatballs with gravy, *161*
    short ribs, coffee-braised, *13*
    short ribs, grilled Korean-style, *89*
    wagyu tartare with oyster cream, corn pudding, and tomatoes, *115*
beets
    in Southern veggie poke, *237*
    in squash blossom salad, *143*
Bengtsson, Emma, *20–27*
berbere-smoked salmon with sweet potato waffles, *163–65*
bhel puri, *37*
bibimbap, *99*

bibingka, banana, *133*
black-eyed peas, in winter melon soup, *109*
borekas, feta, *181*
Boulud, Daniel, *73*
branzino wrapped in grape leaves with muhammara, *151*
breadcrumbs, za'atar, *149*
breads and dough
    corn empanadas, *119*
    egg noodles, *95*
    feta borekas, *181*
    geoduck tartelettes, *45–47*
    ham and cheese piroške, *215*
    hand-torn noodles with cumin lamb, *205*
    Korean sweet pastry, *171*
    lulu pizza, *121*
    naanzanella, *37*
    papdi chips, *39*
    pegao norteño, *59*
breakfast
    pancake stack cake, *217–19*
    teff pancakes, *11*
Brooklyn, New York, *152–57*
Bruner-Yang, Erik, *28–33*
burdock root in pork miso soup, *187*

C

cabbage, asazuke pickles, *19*
cakes. *See also* pancakes
    banana layer, with vanilla cream and candied walnuts, *199*
Cambodia, *244–49*
cantaloupe granita, panna cotta with, *231–33*
carrots
    asazuke pickles, *19*
    in bibimbap, *99*
    in coffee-braised brisket, *179*
    with coffee-braised short ribs, *13*
    in curry-braised lamb belly, *225*
    in pork miso soup, *187*
celtuce, *75–77*
ceviche
    coconut, *145*
    nikkei, *57*
    sea buckthorn aguachile, *191*
Chang, David, *167*
Charleston, South Carolina, *234–39*
charred sweet potatoes with elecampane cream and honey gastrique, *157*
Chase, Leah, *79*
Chauhan, Maneet, *7, 34–41*
cheesecakes, Mykonos, *137–39*
chèvre cheesecake mousse, *137–39*
Chicago, Illinois, *48–53, 106–11*
chicken
    cilantro rice congee, *127*
    crispy soy, *111*
    kara age (fried), *185*
    lala wings, *209*
chickpeas

    with spicy pork lettuce wraps, *105*
    in tomato sauce, *149*
chili sauce, sweet, *125*
chimichurri, *89*
China, *106–15, 206–11, 234–39*
chutneys
    mint, *37, 197*
    tamarind, *37, 39–41*
cilantro rice chicken congee, *127*
clams, littleneck, in coquilles St. Hugues, *63*
coconut beef curry, *239*
coconut ceviche, *145*
coconut cream, *145*
coconut milk-marinated pork with rice, *249*
coffee
    -braised brisket, *179*
    -braised short ribs, *13*
Colombia, *72–77*
congee, cilantro rice chicken, *127*
coquilles St. Hugues, *63*
coriander, Vietnamese, with shrimp and sweet onions, *51*
corn
    empanadas with spicy jam, *119*
    pudding, *115*
    in Southern veggie poke, *237*
couscous with summer vegetables and caramelized tomato, *175*
crab, Dungeness, egg noodles with, *95*
crab fat, *95*
cream cheese soufflé, *137–39*
Crenn, Dominique, *42–47*
Creole dishes, *81–85*
crispy rice lettuce wraps, *125*
crispy soy chicken, *111*
cucumbers
    asazuke pickles, *19*
    with gravlax, *23–24*
    in herb salad, *205*
    pickled, *53*
    in pico de gallo, *39–41*
    salsa, *191*
cumin lace, *59*
curry
    -braised lamb belly, *225*
    coconut beef, *239*
curry paste, for lamb belly, *225*
custard, steamed egg, *169*

D

Dallas, Texas, *8–13*
Dang, Thai, *48–53*
dashi, *17*
Delgado, Carlos, *54–59*
desserts
    banana bibingka, *133*
    banana layer cake with vanilla cream and candied walnuts, *199*
    Korean sweet pastry, *171*
    Mykonos cheesecake, *137–39*

panna cotta with cantaloupe
granita, *231–33*
smoked honey yogurt with whey snow and
white grape syrup, *71*
dips
charred scallion, *81*
muhammara, *151*
duck, vanilla-cured breasts with butter and
apple, *69*
Dufour, Hugue, *60–65*
Dufresne, Wylie, *207, 211*
dumplings, lamb, *59*

E

easy bibimbap for home, *99*
eggplants, in Israeli couscous with summer
vegetables and caramelized tomato, *175*
eggs
braised, in coffee-braised brisket, *179*
cured, in ceviche nikkei, *57*
steamed custard, *169*
Turkish, with chickpeas and garlic
labneh, *149*
elecampane cream, *157*
empanadas, corn, with spicy jam, *119*
epazote leaves, *193*
Ethiopia, *8–13, 158–65*

F

fennel-tomato sauce, *155*
feta
borekas, *181*
ham and cheese piroške, *215*
fish
branzino wrapped in grape leaves with
muhammara, *151*
ceviche nikkei, *57*
coconut ceviche, *145*
fried fillets with mango salad, *247*
grilled whole, with tomato-fennel
sauce, *155*
salmon, berbere-smoked, with sweet
potato waffles *163–65*
salmon, grilled, *53*
salmon gravlax, *23–24*
salmon ochazuke, *17*
sea buckthorn aguachile with cucumber
and kampachi, *191*
sour fish soup, *203*
striped bass moné, mole verdi, *193*
France, *42–47*
Fresno chiles, *89*
fried fish fillets with mango salad, *247*
furikake, *57, 237*

G

Galicia, Diego, *66–71*
geoduck tartelettes, *45–47*
glaze, sweet-and-sour, *223*
gochujang, *99, 105*
granita, cantaloupe, *231–33*
grape leaves, branzino wrapped in, *151*
gravlax with watermelon, cucumber, peas,
and lovage, *23–24*
grilled Korean-style short ribs with Fresno
pepper chimichurri and yogurt, *89*
grilled salmon and snow fungus salad with
Vietnamese herbs, *53*
grilled whole fish with tomato-fennel
sauce, *155*
grits, *83–85*
Gutierrez, Cesar, *72–77*

H

ham and cheese piroške, *215*
hand-torn noodles with cumin lamb, *205*
Helga's meatballs with gravy, *161*
herbes salées, *63*
herbs, Vietnamese, *53*
hoetteok, *171*
hoja santa leaves, *193*
honey yogurt, smoked, with whey snow
and white grape syrup, *71*
honey-vinegar gastrique reduction, *157*
Houston, Texas, *140–45*
hush puppies, takoyaki, *31*

I

India, *34–41*
iru, *243*
Israel, *172–81*
Israeli couscous with summer vegetables
and caramelized tomato, *175*

J

jams and preserves
lingonberry, *161*
raspberry, *217–19*
spicy, *119*
Japan, *14–19, 182–87*
jicamas, in ceviche nikkei, *57*

Jimmy Nardello peppers, *95*
Jung, Jae-Eun, *78–85*

K

Kampachi tuna, *191*
katsuobushi, *17, 19, 31, 75–77, 115*
Keller, Thomas, *97, 129, 221*
Kim, Ann, *86–89*
kimchi, *105*
tomato, *81*
kombu, *17, 19, 57, 75–77*
Korean sweet pastry, *171*

L

labneh, garlic, *149*
lala wings, *209*
Lamagna, Carlo, *90–95*
lamb
cumin, hand-torn noodles with, *205*
curry-braised belly, *225*
keema papdi nachos, *39–41*
pegao norteño, *59*
rosemary-roasted leg of, with mint
chutney, *197*
Laos, *122–27*
Lee, Corey, *96–101*
Lee, Edward, *7, 102–5*
Lee, Johnny, *106–11*
lemon yogurt, *39–41*
lettuce, little gem, with pistachio and
herbs, *229*
lettuce wraps
crispy rice, *125*
spicy pork, *105*
Lewis, Robbie, *129*
Lexington, Kentucky, *102–5*
lingonberry preserves, *161*
little gem lettuce with pistachio and herbs, *229*
lobster, in coquilles St. Hugues, *63*
Los Angeles, California, *106–11, 128–33*
lovage
aïoli, *75–77*
with gravlax, *23–24*
Lu, Binhong, *112–15*
Lulu, the, *121*
lumpia, sea urchin, *131*

M

Mallmann, Francis, *153*
mango salad, fried fish fillets with, *247*

meatballs with gravy, Helga's, *161*
melon, winter, *109*
Mexico, *66–71, 140–51, 188–93, 226–33*
milk crumble, *231–33*
Minneapolis, Minnesota, *86–95*
mint chutney, *37, 197*
miso
    berbere-smoked salmon with sweet
        potato waffles, *163–65*
    -mushroom purée, *223*
    pork soup (tonjiru), *187*
mitmita, *163–65*
mole verde, *193*
Mom's noodles: egg noodles with
    Dungeness crab, crab fat, and peppers, *95*
Moreira, Daniela, *116–21*
mousseline reduction, *45–47*
mozzarella, in ham and cheese piroške, *215*
muhammara, *151*
mushrooms, button, miso-mushroom
    purée, *223*
mushrooms, enoki, in steamed egg
    custard, *169*
mushrooms, shiitake
    in bibimbap, *99*
    in steamed egg custard, *169*
    in winter melon soup, *109*
mussels, in winter melon soup, *109*
My Dad's pork adobo, *93*
My Mom's coffee-braised brisket, *179*
Mykonos, The, *137–39*

N

naan, *37*
naanzanella, *37*
Nashville, Tennessee, *34–41*
New Orleans, Louisiana, *172–75, 240–43*
New York, New York, *20–27, 72–85, 158–65,
    188–93, 200–233*
New Zealand, *194–99*
Nigeria, *240–43*
Nolintha, Vansana, *122–27*
noodles, egg, with Dungeness crab, *95*
noodles, hand-torn, with cumin lamb, *205*
nuoc cham, ginger, *53*

O

Oakland, California, *244–49*
Obraitis, Sarah, *61*
ochazuke, *17*
octopus, takoyaki hush puppies, *31*
okra and shrimp pancakes with charred
    scallion dipping sauce, *81*
Olalia, Charles, *128–33*
Olvera, Enrique, *189*

Ong, Pichet, *134–39*
onions
    in beef curry, *239*
    in coffee-braised brisket, *179*
    in steamed plantain cakes, *243*
onions, pearl, with pickled pork tongue, *65*
onions, red, in ceviche nikkei, *57*
onions, sweet, with shrimp and Vietnamese
    coriander, *51*
onions, white, in pegao norteño, *59*
onions, yellow
    with coffee-braised short ribs, *13*
    in Israeli couscous with summer
        vegetables and caramelized
        tomato, *175*
Ortega, Hugo, *140–45*
oysters
    cream, *115*
    with uni, *33*

P

pancakes
    shrimp and okra with charred scallion
        dipping sauce, *81*
    stack cake, *217–19*
    teff, *11*
panna cotta with cantaloupe granita, *231–33*
papdi chips, *39–41*
pastry, Korean sweet, *171*
Patterson, Daniel, *129*
peach-tomato salad, *83–85*
peas, English, with gravlax, *23–24*
peas, sugar snap, and spring barley, *25–27*
pegao norteño, *59*
peppers
    Fresno chiles, *89*
    Jimmy Nardello, *95*
    red bell, in steamed plantain cakes, *243*
Peru, *54–59*
Philadelphia, Pennsylvania, *166–71*
Philippines, the, *90–95, 128–33, 220–25*
Piattoni, Norberto, *152–57*
pickled pork tongue, *65*
pickles, asazuke, *19*
pico de gallo, *39–41*
pineapple gel, *45–47*
piroške, ham and cheese, *215*
pistachios, little gem lettuce with
    herbs and, *229*
pizza, lulu, *121*
plantain cakes, steamed (ukpo ogede), *243*
plantains, black, steamed cakes, *243*
poke, Southern veggie, *237*
ponzu sauce, *57, 75–77*
pork
    adobo, *93*
    coconut milk-marinated, with rice, *249*
    ham and cheese piroške, *215*
    Helga's meatballs with gravy, *161*
    lettuce wraps, spicy, *105*

miso soup (tonjiru), *187*
    pickled tongue, *65*
    in sea urchin lumpia, *131*
    soy and sugarcane-glazed grilled chops
        and tomato-peach salad, *83–85*
potatoes, new, in curry-braised lamb
    belly, *225*
potatoes, Yukon gold
    in beef curry, *239*
    in coquilles St. Hugues, *63*
    salad, with anchovy, *101*
purslane florets, in squash blossom
    salad, *143*

Q

Quebec, Canada, *60–65*
Queens, New York, *60–65*

R

radishes
    daikon, in pork miso soup, *187*
    watermelon, in squash blossom salad, *143*
Raleigh, North Carolina, *123–27*
ramp oil, *25–27*
raspberry jam, *217–19*
Reggianito cheese, *121*
rice dishes
    banana bibingka, *133*
    bibimbap, *99*
    cilantro rice chicken congee, *127*
    coconut beef curry, *239*
    coconut milk-marinated pork, *249*
    crispy rice lettuce wraps, *125*
    curry-braised lamb belly, *225*
    fried fish fillets with mango salad, *247*
    ochazuke, *17*
    pork adobo, *93*
    shrimp with sweet onions and Vietnamese
        coriander, *51*
    Southern veggie poke, *237*
rice flour cake, *137–39*
Ripert, Eric, *79*
rosemary-roasted leg of lamb and mint
    chutney, *197*

S

salads
    herb, *205, 223*
    little gem lettuce with pistachio and
        herbs, *229*

mango, *247*
potato, with anchovy, *101*
snow fungus, with grilled salmon and Vietnamese herbs, *53*
squash blossom, *143*
tomato-peach, *83–85*
salmon
belly with sweet-and-sour glaze, miso-mushroom purée, and herb salad, *223*
berbere-smoked, with sweet potato waffles, *163–65*
gravlax, *23–24*
grilled, and snow fungus salad with Vietnamese herbs, *53*
ochazuke, *17*
salsa, cucumber, *191*
salted caramel sauce, *231–33*
Samuelsson, Marcus, *7, 158–65*
San Antonio, Texas, *66–71*
San Francisco, California, *42–47, 96–101, 146–51*
sauces
charred scallion dipping, *81*
mole verde, *193*
ponzu, *57, 75–77*
salted caramel, *231–33*
Sriracha-honey, *209*
sweet chili, *125*
tomato, *149*
tomato-fennel, *155*
walnut, *151*
sausage and shrimp stir-fry, *211*
scallions
in bibimbap, *99*
in ceviche nikkei, *57*
in mango salad with fried fish fillets, *247*
in pegao norteño, *59*
scarred-scallion dipping sauce, *81*
in takoyaki hush puppies, *31*
scallops
in coquilles St. Hugues, *63*
with ponzu-poached butternut squash, *75–77*
in winter melon soup, *109*
sea beans in coquilles St. Hugues, *63*
sea buckthorn aguachile with cucumber and kampachi, *191*
sea urchin lumpia, *131*
seafood
coquilles St. Hugues, *63*
Dungeness crab, egg noodles with, *95*
geoduck tartelettes, *45–47*
octopus takoyaki hush puppies, *31*
oysters with uni, *33*
scallops with ponzu-poached butternut squash, *75–77*
sea urchin lumpia, *131*
shrimp and sausage stir-fry, *211*
shrimp with sweet onions and Vietnamese coriander, *51*
steamed egg custard, *169*
winter melon soup, *109*
Seattle, Washington, *182–87*
Serbia, *212–19*

Serpico, Peter, *166–71*
shallots
in butternut squash purée, *75–77*
in hand-torn oodles with cumin lamb, *205*
in mango salad with fried fish fillets, *247*
Shaoxing wine, *203, 209, 211*
Shaya, Alon, *172–75*
shichimi togarashi, *185, 187*
shishito peppers, *211*
shiso leaves, *99, 105*
short ribs
coffee-braised, *13*
grilled Korean-style, *89*
shrimp
in coquilles St. Hugues, *63*
and okra pancakes with charred scallion dipping sauce, *81*
and sausage stir-fry, *211*
in sea urchin lumpia, *131*
in steamed egg custard, *169*
with sweet onions and Vietnamese coriander, *51*
smoked honey yogurt with whey snow and white grape syrup, *71*
snacks, *215*
corn empanadas with spicy jam, *119*
feta borekas, *181*
sea urchin lumpia, *131*
takoyaki hush puppies, *31*
snow fungus, *53*
snow peas and spring barley, *25–27*
Solomonov, Michael, *176–81*
Soma, Mutsuko, *182–87*
Soto-Innes, Daniela, *7, 188–93*
soups
pork miso (tonjiru), *187*
sour fish, *203*
winter melon, *109*
sour fish soup, *203*
South Korea, *78–85, 86–89, 96–105, 166–71, 200–205*
Southern veggie poke, *237*
soy and sugarcane-glazed grilled pork chops and tomato-peach salad, *83–85*
soy bean sprouts, in bibimbap, *99*
spicy pork lettuce wraps, *105*
spinach
in bibimbap, *99*
puréed, *25–27*
spring barley and vegetables, *25–27*
squash blossom salad, *143*
squashes
butternut, ponzu-poached, scallops with, *75–77*
kobocha, in pegao norteño, *59*
squid, in winter melon soup, *109*
Sriracha-honey sauce, *209*
steamed egg custard, *169*
steamed plantain cakes, *243*
Stone, Jeremiah, *227*
strawberries in naanzanella, *137*
striped bass moné, mole verde, *193*
sturgeon, in coquilles St. Hugues, *63*
Sukhendra, Joseph, *194–99*

Sweden, *20–27, 158–65*
sweet potatoes
charred, with elecampane cream and honey gastrique, *157*
waffles, with berbere-smoked salmon, *163–65*
syrup, white grape, *71*

T

Taiwan, *28–33*
takoyaki hush puppies, *31*
tamarind chutney, *37, 39–41*
tartelettes, geoduck, *45–47*
tea, kombu, *17, 19*
teff pancakes, *11*
Tejada, Máximo, *221*
Telfeyan, Kate, *200–205*
Thailand, *134–39, 244–49*
tofu, in pork miso soup, *187*
tomatoes
caramelized, with Israeli couscous and summer vegetables, *175*
-fennel, *155*
kimchi, *81*
in Lulu pizza, *121*
-peach salad, *83–85*
pickled, *25–27*
in pico de gallo, *39–41*
sauce, *149*
tomatoes, cherry
semi-dried, *115*
in Southern veggie poke, *237*
in squash blossom salad, *143*
Tong, Simone, *206–11*
tonjiru, *187*
Tower, Jeremiah, *43*
trei jien, *247*
tuna
ceviche nikkei, *57*
coconut ceviche, *145*
sea buckthorn aguachile, *191*
Turkey, *146–51*
Turkish eggs with chickpeas and garlic labneh, *149*

U

ukpo ogede, *243*
Ultra-Tex 3, *45*
uni
geoduck tartelettes and, *45–47*
oysters with, *33*
sea urchin lumpia, *131*
Urasawa, Hiroyuki, *15*
Uskokovic, Miroslav, *5, 212–19*

V

vanilla
  cream and candied walnuts with banana layer cake, *199*
  -cured duck breasts with butter and apple, *69*
Vaught, Tracy, *141*
vegetable dishes. *See also specific types*
  asazuke pickles, *19*
  bibimbap, *99*
  Southern veggie poke, *237*
  spring barley and, *25–27*
  steamed plantain cakes, *243*
  summer, with Israeli couscous and caramelized tomato, *175*
Vietnam, *48–53*
Villarosa, Harold, *220–25*
vinegar gel, *45–47*
Voltaggio, Brian, *55*
von Hauske Valtierra, Fabián, *226–33*

W

waffles, sweet potato, with berbere-smoked salmon, *163–65*
wagyu beef tartare with oyster cream, corn, pudding, and tomatoes, *115*
walnuts
  candied, banana layer cake with vanilla cream and, *199*
  in pancake stack cake, *217–19*
  sauce, *151*
Wang, Shuai, *234–39*
Washington, D.C., *28–33, 54–59, 112–21, 134–39*
watermelon with gravlax, *23–24*
Wey, Tunde, *240–43*
whipped cream, *45–47*
white grape syrup, *71*
winter melon soup, *109*
Wiseheart, Andrew, *195*
World Central Kitchen, *5*

Y

yogurt
  garlic labneh, *149*
  lemon, *39–41*
  for naanzanella, *37*
  smoked honey, *71*
Yun, Nite, *244–49*

Z

za'atar breadcrumbs, *149*
zucchinis
  in bibimbap, *99*
  in Israeli couscous with summer vegetables and caramelized tomato, *175*
  in squash blossom salad, *143*

Acknowledgments

Our heartfelt gratitude goes to: the wonderful Holly LaDue at Prestel Publishing, who thoughtfully stewarded this book from conception to completion. To Denise Sommer and Connie Koch for graphic design magic. To the photographers from coast to coast, especially Peter Hurley and Melissa Hom. To Kirstin Donnelley, Lauren Salkeld, and Ayesha Wadhawan for eagle eyes. And we give thanks foremost to Jan and Marica Vilcek, founders of the Vilcek Foundation. Their leadership and lives have rightly been called "an antidote to xenophobia" and we hope this book will be, too.

Photography Credits

Chris Gillett: 8, 10, 12, 14–15, 16, 18, 66–67, 68, 70, 140–41, 142, 144, 194–95, 196, 198; **Melissa Hom:** 20–21, 22, 26, 60, 62, 64, 78, 80, 82, 84, 176, 190, 192, 206, 208, 210, 212–13, 214, 216, 218, 220, 222, 224, 232; **John Taggart:** 28–29, 30, 32, 112, 114, 116, 118, 120, 134, 136, 166, 168, 170; **Emily B. Hall:** 34–35, 36, 38, 40; **Peter Hurley:** 42–43, 44, 48–49, 50, 52, 72–73, 74, 76, 96–97, 98, 100, 152–53, 154, 156, 158–59, 160, 162, 200, 202, 204; **Eric Thayer:** 54–55, 56, 58; **The Restaurant Project:** 86; **Rachael Crew:** 88; **Levy Moroshan:** 90–91, 92, 94; **Elaine Zelker:** 102, 104; **Gavin Hill:** 106, 108, 110, 128, 130, 132; **Todd Dring:** 122, 124, 126; **Karaminder Ghuman:** 146, 148, 150, 244, 246, 248; **The Vilcek Foundation:** 164; **Rush Jagoe:** 172, 174; **Michael Persico:** 178, 180; **Olli Tumelius:** 182, 184, 186; **Maureen Evans:** 188; **Matty Yangwoo Kim:** 226, 228, 230; **Sully Sullivan:** 234, 236, 238; **L. Kasimu Harris:** 240, 242

Recipe Credits

The publisher wishes to thank the following for graciously allowing us to reproduce recipes and/or photographs.

Fabián von Hauske Valtierra: Adapted from A Very Serious Cookbook by Jeremiah Stone and Fabián von Hauske. © 2018 Phaidon Press Limited.

Michael Solomonov: Excerpted from Zahav by Michael Solomonov and Steven Cook. Copyright © 2015 by Michael Solomonov and Steven Cook. Photos by Michael Persico. Used by permission of Houghton Mifflin Harcourt. All rights reserved.

Alon Shaya: Adapted from Shaya: An Odyssey of Food, My Journey Back to Israel. Copyright © 2018 by Alon Shaya.

VILCEK FOUNDATION

Prestel Publishing Ltd.
14-17 Wells Street
London W1T 3PD

Prestel Publishing
900 Broadway, Suite 603
New York, NY 10003

Library of Congress Cataloging-in-Publication Data

Names: Langholtz, Gabrielle, author. | Kinsel, Rick, author.
Title: A place at the table : new American recipes from the nation's top
   foreign-born chefs / Gabrielle Langholtz and Rick Kinsel.
Description: Munich ; New York : Prestel, [2019] | Includes index.
Identifiers: LCCN 2019003403 | ISBN 9783791385181 (hardcover)
Subjects: LCSH: Cooking, American. | LCGFT: Cookbooks. | Recipes.
Classification: LCC TX715 .L27756 2019 | DDC 641.5973--dc23
LC record available at https://lccn.loc.gov/2019003403

A CIP catalogue record for this book is available from the British Library.

Editorial direction: Holly La Due
Design and layout: Ahoy Studios
Production management: Anjali Pala
Copyediting: Lauren Salkeld
Proofreading: Monica Parcell
Index: Marilyn Bliss

Verlagsgruppe Random House FSC® N001967
Printed on the FSC®-certified paper

Printed in China

ISBN 978-3-7913-8518-1

www.prestel.com